Accolades for
Extreme Paranormal Investigations

D1532372

EXTREME
PARANORMAL
INVESTIGATIONS

About the Author

Marcus F. Griffin's sixth birthday present was a coffin built by his father at the request of young Marcus, who piled books and stuffed animals on top of it of every night so he'd be awakened if anything tried to crawl out of it while he was sleeping. The rest, as they say, is history.

Thanks to childhood encounters with unexplainable supernatural events, Marcus was driven to study the mysteries of a multitude of worlds; as a result, he has been a student and teacher of metaphysics, spirituality, and the paranormal for more than twenty-nine years.

He is author of *Advancing the Witches' Craft: Aligning Your Magical Spirit Through Meditation, Exploration, and Initiation of the Self*; a literary horror novel, *Slaughter*; and a nonfiction spiritual tome, *Tribe: Tending the Fires of the Great Spirit Within*.

An active member of the Horror Writers Association, Marcus is also a regular contributor to the Llewellyn annuals and writes a monthly feature column for Ghostvillage .com. He lives with his wife in northern Indiana, in a haunted home located on their sanctuary, which is known as Nevermore Gardens.

Please visit his website, www.marcusfgriffin.com. Marcus can also be contacted by e-mail, at marcusfgriffin @comcast.net, or you can follow him on Twitter, where he tweets as @MarcusFGriffin.

Marcus F. Griffin
Foreword by Jeff Belanger

EXTREME
PARANORMAL
I N V E S T I G A T I O N S

The Blood Farm Horror,
The Legend of Primrose Road,
and Other Disturbing Hauntings

Llewellyn Publications
Woodbury, Minnesota

FIRST EDITION
First Printing, 2011

Cover design by Lisa Novak
Cover images: clouds © iStockphoto.com/Jeka Gorbunov; house © iStockphoto
    .com/Shaun Lowe
Interior art © Art Explosion

Llewellyn is a registered trademark of Llewellyn Worldwide Ltd.

Library of Congress Cataloging-in-Publication Data
Griffin, Marcus F., 1960-
   Extreme paranormal investigations : the Blood Farm horror, the legend of Primrose Road, and other disturbing hauntings / Marcus F. Griffin ; foreword by Jeff Belanger. — 1st ed.
      p.   cm.
   Includes bibliographical references.
   ISBN 978-0-7387-2697-7
1. Ghosts—Middle West. 2. Witches in Search of the Paranormal (Organization)
I. Title.
   BF1472.U6G76 2011
   133.10973—dc23
                          2011020445

Llewellyn Publications
A Division of Llewellyn Worldwide Ltd.
2143 Wooddale Drive
Woodbury, MN 55125-2989
www.llewellyn.com

Printed in the United States of America

For my son, Logan, who proved to me that even things long thought dead can still be brought back to life.

Contents

Foreword

The paranormal has called to humanity for as long as there have been people roaming our planet. These deep mysteries beckon us to search our world, our universe, and our souls for answers. Today, exploring the unexplained is in vogue. Many television shows glorify the pursuit, and people are coming to the paranormal table from all walks of life, because maybe they've had an encounter—or more likely it's because they want to have incredible experiences and find some answers. The reasons are not what's most important, as long as they do come to the table.

When I began corresponding with Marcus Griffin back in 2004, we discussed many Witchy subjects, but mostly we talked about ghosts, spirit contact, and how people are investigating supernatural claims. Though Griffin blames me in the introduction to this book for starting his group, he is the one who should get most of the blame ... *err* ... credit.

There has been a trend in recent years to try to make paranormal research more scientific. It's gotten to the point where some investigators believe their EMF meters and audio recorders more than they believe their own senses. The ghost experience has always been a sensory event. We see, hear, feel, and smell something we can't explain. To ignore our senses is to ignore our ghosts. What I love about the WISP approach is its return to the esoteric and the magical roots of the paranormal … but with an appreciation for new techniques and technologies.

We are all a product of our upbringing, and that includes our religious belief system. To ignore those roots is not only impossible, but it's a disservice to ourselves. If you're a Christian, bring your Christianity to paranormal investigation. Wear a cross for protection. Use holy water if you feel afraid or threatened. Pray if you want guidance. If you're a Witch, you also have tools available to you. Casting a circle. Casting a spell for protection or guidance. Using amulets or crystals to try and draw in spirit contact. Just come to the table as you are.

WISP has done that. They began tackling well-known paranormal cases like Chicago's Resurrection Mary and more obscure haunts like the ghost of Belle Gunness in Indiana. At first, Griffin's approach was all esoteric, but soon he and his group found a place for audio recorders and other devices made popular by modern-day paranormal investigators. They got results: unexplained voices on their audio recordings and strange anomalies on their photographs. They believe their results, and they believe their senses.

You're about to embark on a journey with some Witches who bring a lot of experience and personality to the paranormal. You have the opportunity not only to explore the cases they've worked on, but also to see the inner workings of a paranormal research group. It's a wild ride. WISP plumbs the depths of these big questions and touches the faces of those on the other side. Grab your broom, your black Witchy hat, and your EMF meter. You're about to go ghost hunting with WISP!

—Jeff Belanger, founder of Ghostvillage.com, host of *30 Odd Minutes*, and author of *Picture Yourself Legend Tripping*

Introduction

The Pack in Black: Who Are WISP?

Dressed in clothing blacker than midnight and armed with an assortment of high-tech ghost-hunting gear, four powerful Witches stride into the night to make contact with the entities of the netherworld. Their occult skills are unmatched, their bravery unshakable. Like the Four Horsemen of the Apocalypse, they ... umm ... excuse me .... "Yes, dear? But—but, are you sure? *Damn!*" Sorry about that. My wife was scolding me for overdramatizing.

Witches in Search of the Paranormal (WISP) was formed in October 2004, with the express purpose of studying the connection between Witchcraft and the paranormal. Author extraordinaire and Ghostvillage.com owner Jeff Belanger had contacted me through our mutual publisher and asked if I would be willing to write a monthly feature for his website, focusing on this connection. After carefully thinking about Jeff's offer (yes, it's all his fault), I realized that the only way to properly study the connection between Witchcraft and the paranormal was by performing field research. Thus, team WISP sprang into existence.

Now that you know the *why*, let's take a look at the *how*.

When WISP first began investigating the paranormal, we were metaphysical purists. In other words, in the beginning we used no ghost-hunting gear of any kind and relied instead solely on our wits and esoteric skills to conduct investigations. We quickly learned, however, that a marriage of metaphysics and science—high-tech gear added to our occult skills—was necessary to conduct fair and objective investigations and collect evidence of paranormal activity. Thus a new breed of investigator was born: Witches armed with experience and technology rather than crystal balls and magic wands.

Individual members of WISP began studying metaphysics and all things esoteric in our early twenties. After the four members of the future team met at a Pagan festival in northern Indiana in the summer of 1999, we merged our respective covens and spent the next decade studying and teaching advanced techniques in Witchcraft. As a team, WISP members have been performing paranormal investigations for more than seven years, and we are self-funded. During those seven years, WISP has investigated some of the Midwest's most famous paranormal legends and has helped many individuals and families with their own ghosts and hauntings. As intriguing as investigating well-known paranormal legends is, above all else helping others is what keeps the team motivated.

WISP's scientific and metaphysical investigatory methods will be revealed in depth as our strange stories unfold, but for now let's take a few moments to meet the individual members of the team and gain deeper insight into our personal motivations for investigating paranormal activity.

Declassified:
Team WISP Member Profiles

Marcus F. Griffin: Lead investigator and founder of WISP Paranormal

Technological specialty: Recording and examining audio evidence of paranormal activity

Metaphysical specialties: Energy manipulation and dispatching malevolent entities

Ryan Hayward

Background and core beliefs: I, Marcus, grew up in a haunted house, and at a very early age I experienced frequent encounters with unexplainable paranormal events. As a result of these early life encounters, I was driven to discover and explore a multitude of worlds. At twenty-three years of age, I began studying the practice of Witchcraft. Once I became comfortably adept at my practice, I went on to explore and study all things esoteric. I believe that using my metaphysical skills to examine and investigate paranormal activity is the next logical step on my spiritual path, and I intend to continue following this path until it leads to the height of its potential. I am drawn neither to prove nor disprove the existence of otherworldly entities, but merely to discover how to unlock the doors and bring the worlds of the living and the dead closer together than ever before. I also believe that we humans are as much "ghosts" in the world of the dead as they are ghosts in ours.

• • • •

Amber Morgan: Investigator and scribe

Technological specialty: Recording video evidence of paranormal activity

Metaphysical specialties: Automatic writing, raising energy, cleansing energies

Background and core beliefs: At a very young age, Amber had encounters with the paranormal, beginning shortly after the death of her older sister. Amber believes that the ghost of her deceased sister "visited" her many times during her childhood, scolding and giving advice. Amber's interest in the paranormal resurfaced later in life during her study of Paganism. During her studies she learned about house cleansings, and conducted many such cleansings during her time as a student and later as a teacher. When Amber joined WISP, it was to find a new way to study the paranormal. She was fascinated and enthused when she discovered that WISP would incorporate both scientific and metaphysical methodologies into its investigations to find the most efficient way to communicate with the spirit world. Amber, who is married to Sam, is also the scribe of the team and records accounts of all metaphysical procedures and paranormal activity captured during WISP's investigations.

• • • •

Sam Leonhart: Investigator

Technological specialty: Electronics wizard

Metaphysical specialties: Psychometry, psychology, energy manipulation

Background and core beliefs: At an early age, Sam gained experience working with energy through séances he conducted with family members. Later on in life he studied Paganism and, once he attained a sufficient level of proficiency, co-founded two covens that practiced Wicca. Sam's studies eventually led to his Priesthood, and since his ordination, Sam has performed numerous ceremonies such as handfastings, funeral rites, baptisms, and initiations. Sam believes that joining team WISP was an excellent opportunity to continue his metaphysical studies and provided him with what he feels is the perfect vehicle for proving or disproving accounts of paranormal activity. Sam believes that paranormal activity does in fact exist, but he is desirous of collecting hard evidence to share with others—skeptics and believers alike. He also believes that we are all connected through the energies that are universal to this, and every other, plane of existence.

• • • •

Becca B. Griffin: Investigator, photographer, videographer

Technological specialties: Collecting photographic evidence, historian

Metaphysical specialties: Energy manipulation, astrology, ritualist

Background and core beliefs: In her youth, Becca experienced many paranormal events that nurtured her natural curiosity for all things unseen and unexplained. Later in life she discovered that her grandmother possessed psychic abilities, and Becca soon discovered that she herself possessed these abilities. While in her mid-twenties, Becca began privately studying Witchcraft and Paganism, which eventually led her into the Priestesshood. Along with her husband, Marcus, she is the co-founder of a Pagan church and teaching coven in northern Indiana. Becca's interest in a comprehensive search for the paranormal began after the death of her mother in 1990. She believes that joining WISP was the next logical step for her to take in her desire to learn as much as she can in her lifetime.

Now that you've met the team, let's take the time to learn more about the metaphysical techniques that WISP utilizes to study the connection between Witchcraft and the paranormal.

The Witchcraft Connection, Part I

Practitioners of Witchcraft are often viewed as having a deeper connection to the supernatural than the average person. Is this true? When it comes to hunting ghosts and investigating paranormal activity, does the Witch's supernatural connection give him or her an advantage over common paranormal investigators who incorporate only scientific methods in their investigations?

In the investigations that follow, WISP uses all of the metaphysical and scientific tools and skills at our disposal to examine the mysteries of the paranormal and discover for ourselves the depth and breadth of the connection between Witchcraft and the paranormal. Yes, science plays a crucial role in WISP's ability to collect and examine evidence of paranormal entities, just as our instincts and metaphysical skills are crucial in making contact with these entities—but beyond the technological gadgetry, we use advanced metaphysical skills and techniques to bring the worlds of the living and the dead closer together.

The primary metaphysical tool we use to accomplish this goal is commonly known among occult practitioners as *energy manipulation*. While an adept practitioner can use energy manipulation for a variety of reasons and in many different circumstances, WISP uses very specific applications targeted at communicating with the dead. These applications include but are not limited to:

- Creating a protective boundary
- Erecting an energy wall to keep non-indigenous entities away from an investigation site and keep indigenous entities contained
- Lighting up a specific area with energy to open spirit communication
- Opening a portal (such as a vortex) by punching a hole between the worlds of the living and the dead
- Fending off troublesome poltergeists or malevolent spirits

- Creating and maintaining a concentrated energy field on which ghosts can feed, allowing them to make stronger and more frequent contact
- Forcing materialization and/or verbal communication with paranormal entities

One of WISP's core beliefs is that an investigator shouldn't enter into an investigation to "prove" or "disprove" paranormal activity. We believe that such a mindset can be detrimental to an investigation. This isn't to say, of course, that a natural explanation of allegedly paranormal phenomena shouldn't be sought out first. Natural causes should always be ruled out before a paranormal cause is even considered. But in our opinion, far too many paranormal investigators set out to "debunk" paranormal phenomena. This can be every bit as harmful as entering into an investigation with the certainty that ghosts are lurking around every corner.

Keeping an *open mind* to any and all possibilities, both natural and supernatural, is critical when conducting a fair and uncontaminated investigation. What do I mean? Try this: Picture in your mind a group of paranormal investigators entering a supposedly haunted location with the purpose of debunking possibly paranormal activity. What's going to happen? Pretty much the same thing that would happen if a team of scientists entered your house and attempted to debunk your existence. In other words, imagine that these scientists are arriving to prove that *you're not real. You don't exist.* Picture this team of scientists repeatedly *telling you that you don't exist.* Exactly what do you think is going to happen?

I'm no roadside psychic, but I'm going to guess that two of the most likely scenarios would be that you're either going to cower whimpering in the corner or get so pissed off that you slap one or more of them across the face. Now picture this same team of scientists entering into your home with open minds, not attempting to prove or disprove anything, but simply to observe. Ahh. Now I'm guessing a completely different scene is unfolding in your mind at this very second. Finally, picture in your mind a team of paranormal investigators entering a supposedly haunted location with the same open minds. If I were the ghost in question, I'd probably be much more apt to act naturally than I would if this same team of investigators were attempting to deny my presence.

Team WISP's logo is a drawing of a puzzle piece inside of a puzzle piece. That's what we believe the paranormal is—a puzzle within a puzzle. We believe that paranormal activity can never be totally "proved" or "disproved." And therein lies its true beauty. The paranormal is a beautiful mystery, and like any true mystery, it isn't something to be solved or disproved, but enjoyed. The mysteries of our world are what make it interesting. They're what make our lives more magical. To prove my point, ask yourself this: What would be more magical? Watching the six-o'-clock news and seeing a team of reporters filming a one-hundred-foot-long creature that had washed up on the shores of Loch Ness, or standing on the shore of the loch and imagining what might be swimming below its surface? Yes, proof of such a creature would be a very interesting scientific find, but it would also forever erase a bit of the magic from our world.

EVP

Audio evidence of paranormal activity is very important to WISP's investigations. So important, in fact, that before we delve into the team's adventures, we should take a brief moment to look at how team WISP classifies EVP, or *electronic voice phenomena*.

Electronic voice phenomena, which many investigators believe to be the voices of the dead captured on audio recorders, are arguably the most intriguing evidence of supernatural activity captured during paranormal investigations. They are also the most frequently found evidence.

What follows are descriptions of the three types of EVP classifications WISP uses when evaluating audio evidence of paranormal activity:

1. **A-class.** A-class EVP are very clear voices that are easily understood by anyone who listens to the recording. A-class EVP do not need to be amplified or cleaned up by a computer program to be understood. They can be clearly heard straight from the recording device.

2. **B-class.** B-class EVP are reasonably easy to hear and understand, but not everyone who listens to the recording may agree on what the voice is saying. Listeners may not be able to make out each and every word being spoken. B-class EVP typically require some degree of amplification and cleaning up by a computer program before they can be understood.

3. **C-class.** C-class EVP are often low-quality recordings that are nearly impossible to understand, even when enhanced by a computer program. C-class EVP are

often no louder than very faint whispers and are barely discernible from background noise.

The Hunt Begins

Now that you know the who, how, and why, we should probably get moving. The hour is growing late and ghosts are on the prowl. The time has come to center our minds, gather our gear, and take our first few steps on the road that leads to the otherworld. This is a road from my youth. We go now to visit Cableline Road.

Prologue:

The Monster of Cableline Road

It seems that for as long as there have been streets, roads, and highways, there have been ghosts haunting them. Perhaps the first legends of haunted roadways were based upon the living rather than the dead: the mystery of the unknown traveler or the uncertainty of who or what might be waiting around the next bend in the road. In my youth, my friends and I would occasionally travel down a stretch of roadway in northern Indiana that was said to be haunted by a ghostly motorcyclist. That stretch of roadway was also burdened by a strange urban legend: *the Monster of Cableline Road*.

The tale of the ghostly motorcyclist is in part based on fact. In the mid-1970s, a motorcyclist was killed on Cableline Road when he ran a stop sign at a high rate of speed and crashed his bike into a tree. He left behind a gruesome reminder of the accident: he hit the tree with such force that the outline of his body was scarred into the tree trunk. I'll never forget the first time I laid eyes upon it. The outline of the dead motorcyclist was so well defined on the tree trunk that it sent chills up and down my spine. It still does to this day. The legend of the ghostly motorcyclist was an integral part of youth, and in no small part fostered my fascination with the paranormal later in life.

The *Monster* of Cableline Road, on the other hand, is a completely different story. I am uncertain as to the origin of this local urban legend, but as I clearly recall, when I was younger, I used to play it for all it was worth. I remember taking many a girlfriend or unsuspecting date for a late-night drive down Cableline Road in hopes of giving them a little scare. My unspoken agenda, of course, was to get the young lady to snuggle up close to me as I slowly drove down Cableline Road reciting the legend of the monster. It usually worked like a charm. Such memories make me wonder just how many of the world's strange tales and ghostly urban legends came into existence for that simple reason: the guy wants to get the girl. Or at least to impress her.

What is it about ghosts and the paranormal that attracts so many of us? Is it the promise of temporary escape from the drudgery and predictability of everyday life? Is it the thrill of possibly experiencing the unknown firsthand? The lure of having an intriguing tale to share with our friends and families? Or is it something even more fundamental? Belief in ghosts and unseen worlds carries a very important spiritual message and a basic psychological need. We need to be reassured that something exists beyond what we can see with our eyes and touch with our hands—to be reassured that, in one form or another, there *is* life after death.

It seems odd to me, as I sit here writing this prologue on a warm, sunlit spring day, that I am drawn to speak of the dark and mysterious world of ghosts and the paranormal. The flowers are in bloom, nature and life surround me, and yet—a secret place deep inside me yearns for midnight and a lonely stretch of haunted highway. I am drawn by the ghost and what my belief in him has to offer—that I will live on after I have left this world. That one day the hunter will become that which he has hunted.

As you begin reading the investigations that follow, you will discover that I have taken a few liberties with the chapter titles in this book. Not all of our investigations are centered on roads and the ghosts that haunt them. But it is always a road that leads us to our destinations. Always, it is a road that becomes a path that leads us deeper and deeper into the realms of the unseen and the unexplained. If the journey of a thousand miles begins with a single step, then, as investigators of the paranormal, we must travel a thousand miles simply to get to step one.

It has been suggested that life is like a highway, and that each and every road we travel brings us closer to our destinies, that each and every exit is a chance for a new experience. At one point in my past, I took an exit on the highway of life that led me into the strange and often bizarre worlds of the occult and the paranormal. And for me, at least, it is far too late to turn back. So allow me to whisk you away into the haunted night and tell you the tale of our strange journey. Travel with us as we walk the long and shadowy roadway into the unknown.

Chapter 1

McClung Road: Belle Gunness and the Blood Farm Horror

Investigation: Former Belle Gunness property

Start date: April 22, 2006

Place: La Porte, Indiana

Who Was Belle Gunness?[1]

Belle Gunness—born Brynhild Paulsdatter Størset in Selbu, Norway, in November 1859—is arguably America's most notorious female serial killer. Gunness is often referred to as *Lady Bluebeard*, and her story was gruesome enough to inspire folklore and folk songs. She is believed to have murdered upwards of forty people during her bloody reign at a La Porte, Indiana, hog farm in the early twentieth century, although to date only twelve bodies and several miscellaneous body parts have been discovered on what was her property. After she purportedly murdered her first two husbands for the insurance money, Belle's modus operandi for finding victims was to place lonely-hearts ads in foreign-language newspapers.

---

1. Some historical background in this chapter was found online, at the Belle Gunness page on the La Porte County Historical Society's website: www.laportecountyhistory.org/belleg1.htm.

> *WANTED—A woman who owns a beauti-*
> *fully located and valuable farm in first-class con-*
> *dition wants a good and reliable man as partner*
> *in same. Some little cash is required, for which*
> *will be furnished first-class security.*[2]

Those who were unfortunate enough to answer Belle's ads were instructed to sell everything they owned and come and stay with her in La Porte. Gunness had discovered an easy way to make money: murder. Only one man who answered her ads made it off her farm alive.

The Bloody History of a Female Serial Killer: Belle Gunness

In the early morning hours of April 28, 1908, a farmhouse located on McClung Road near the outskirts of La Porte burned to the ground. Forty-eight-year-old Belle Gunness owned the farmhouse, which she had lived in since 1901. La Porte County Sheriff Albert Smutzer led the investigation of the fire. When investigators arrived at the scene of the fire and began sifting through the rubble, they made a grisly discovery. Four bodies were found in what remained of the burned-out basement of the farmhouse: the bodies of one adult female and three children.

At first, investigators believed the bodies to be those of Belle Gunness and her three children: Myrtle, age eleven; Lucy, age nine; and Phillip, age five. Sheriff Smutzer discovered that what at first appeared to be a routine investigation

---

2. Source: Promotional brochure furnished by the La Porte County Historical Society for the permanent Belle Gunness exhibit at the society's
   museum.

was anything but. Although the bodies of the three children were soon identified, the body of the woman was missing its head and therefore could not be identified by means of dental records. There was also a problem with the size of the body. Belle Gunness stood approximately 5'9" and weighed in at a hefty 280 pounds, whereas the body in the basement of the burned-out farmhouse was approximated to have stood a mere 5'3" and estimated to have weighed 125 pounds. This was too large a discrepancy to be ignored.

The source of the blaze that destroyed the farmhouse was suspicious as well. In search of answers, Sheriff Smutzer brought in Belle's hired handyman, Ray Lamphere, for questioning. At first Lamphere denied having any knowledge of or involvement with the fire, but an eyewitness reported seeing him fleeing the farm on the morning of the blaze. Lamphere was eventually charged with arson and four counts of murder. While Lamphere was acquitted of the murder charges on November 26, 1908, the jury found him guilty of arson. He contracted tuberculosis while serving his sentence and died in December 1909.

Before he died, though, Lamphere gave an in-depth confession in which he insisted that Belle Gunness had not died in the fire. Lamphere claimed that he had assisted in Belle's escape by taking her to Stillwell, a small town approximately eight miles east of La Porte, where she had caught a train to Chicago. Lamphere confessed to returning to the Gunness property after dropping Belle off in Stillwell and setting fire to the farmhouse in an attempt cover her escape. He further claimed that the headless body discovered in the remains of the farmhouse belonged to a woman from Chicago whom

Belle had hired as a housekeeper several days before the fire. He claimed that Belle had murdered her three children and planted their bodies in the basement of the farmhouse to make it look as though they had been killed in the fire. He further admitted to helping Belle bury, or otherwise dispose of, the bodies of other victims, but denied any involvement in their murders. It is widely believed that Ray Lamphere was in love with Gunness and that he died still pining away for his murderous employer.

The discovery of the bodies of Belle's other victims came about in May 1908, when a man named Asle Helgelien came to La Porte from South Dakota to search for his missing brother, Andrew. Andrew had come to Indiana to meet and, he hoped, marry Belle after answering the ad that she had placed in a Norwegian-language newspaper. Asle had contacted Belle several months earlier inquiring as to the whereabouts of his brother, and Belle had allegedly replied that things hadn't worked out and that Andrew had left her farm. Not believing her story, Asle traveled to La Porte. On May 4, he contacted Sheriff Smutzer and stated his concern that his brother Andrew might have met with foul play at Belle's hands. Asle asked the sheriff for permission to search the Gunness property and possibly do some digging.

There are two different stories as to how Sheriff Smutzer reacted to Asle's request. The first is that the sheriff refused to allow Asle to search the farm, but he did it anyway. The second is that Asle's accusations aroused the sheriff's suspicions and he gave Asle permission to perform a search. Either way, a search of the Gunness farm began. Joe Maxon, who had been one of Belle's hired hands at the time of the fire, pointed out a likely place to dig for bodies. On May 5, 1908, the first body was discovered four feet below ground level. Unfortunately for Asle, it was the body of his brother, Andrew. All told, twelve bodies were eventually unearthed at the Gunness farm. Asle Helgelien had his brother's remains interred at Walker Cemetery (now known as Patton Cemetery) and returned to South Dakota.

The true fate of Belle Gunness is unknown. Did Belle, as some believe, die with her children in an accidental fire? Or did she make a clean getaway, never having paid for her grisly crimes? We may never know. But one thing is certain: the legend of Belle Gunness and the Blood Farm Horror will ring out through the annals of ghostly lore and literature.

Research and Discovery

Team WISP began its investigation of the Belle Gunness murders by traveling to the La Porte County Library, where we found extensive files on the case. The Gunness murder files were such a popular attraction at the library, in fact, that all materials pertaining to Gunness had been concentrated into a single (albeit massive) file folder. Upon receiving the file folder from the librarian, team WISP located an empty table near the back of the library and began the daunting task of sifting through the enormous pile of newspaper clippings, book excerpts, and magazine articles that pertained to the murders. The library's materials dated from as early as 1908 (the year in which the first bodies were discovered) to as recently as 2005.

Among the more interesting materials was a newspaper article from 1931, which reported that the Los Angeles Police

Department believed that they had Belle Gunness in custody. The LAPD had arrested a woman named Esther Carlson on charges of poisoning her eighty-one-year-old employer, August Lindstrom. The article reported that Los Angeles deputy district attorney George Stahlman had contacted La Porte County Sheriff McDonald (first name unknown), stating his suspicions that he believed Esther Carlson to be none other than the notorious Belle Gunness. Oddly, Sheriff McDonald hesitated to act on Stahlman's suspicions and refused to spend the money to send an investigator to California to follow up on the lead until he was provided with more convincing evidence. No further evidence could be provided, and Stahlman's suspicion that Esther Carlson was in fact Belle Gunness was never proved nor disproved. The truth died in prison with Esther Carlson.

One of the main goals of our visit to the La Porte County Library was to discover the exact location of the former Gunness farm. The only thing we knew for certain was that the property was located on McClung Road on the outskirts of the city. By sheer luck, out of the hundreds and hundreds of clippings and newspaper articles we pulled from the file folder, Becca discovered an obscure article that gave a detailed description of the landscape surrounding the former Gunness property. These geographic clues were all we had to work with, as our attempts at locating an exact street address had been an exercise in futility. And so, with clues in hand, we exited the library and headed for McClung Road.

Belle's Old Stalking Grounds

Even though we felt confident that we could locate the former Gunness farm, the geographic clues we possessed as to
the property's whereabouts were certain to push our sleuth-
ing skills to the max. The article that Becca had found stated
that a new, single-story house had been constructed on the
original foundation of Belle's farmhouse and that the house
sat atop the crown of a knoll. The article also described a
curve in the road directly in front of the property and a large
growth of cedar and ash trees. As we drove along McClung
Road, we neared a house that fit the description. Well, it *almost* fit the description. The geography was a match, but the
house was a two-story home, not the single-story home described in the article.

Wondering if we had in fact discovered Belle's property
and the article was wrong, I pulled the van onto the shoulder
of the road and killed the engine. The first thing I noticed
was a large black-and-orange *No Trespassing* sign propped up
inside a front window of the house. This aroused my suspicions even further, and I wondered if the homeowner had
been bothered by Belle Gunness investigators in the past. Uncertain as to whether or not it was a smart idea to knock on
the door, I scanned the neighboring houses in search of any
signs of life. I was delighted to see a young woman playing
with her three children in the front yard of the house right
next door. I told my teammates that I was going to see if the
woman would be willing to talk with me, and pen and note-
pad in hand, I exited the van and walked toward her.

Upon noticing me approaching, the woman greeted me
with a big smile. She rose from her resting spot under a shade

tree and, in true Indiana style, gave me a proper country welcome. I introduced myself as an author doing research for a series of articles about Belle Gunness and asked her if she knew the whereabouts of Belle's property. She said that she thought it was the house next door but wasn't sure, then added that her husband probably knew and that he was in the backyard mowing the grass. She said that she was certain that he would be willing to talk to me about Belle, and that she would gladly "go and fetch him" for me.

I thanked her and told her that I would be most grateful. The woman disappeared behind the house and several minutes later returned with her husband, who had a very apprehensive look on his face. When I introduced myself and explained what I was up to, the young man got the proverbial shit-eating grin on his face. He said that even though he didn't know very much, he would be glad to tell me what he knew. The house next door, he said, was indeed the Gunness property, and most of the surrounding area had been her farm. When I asked him about the discrepancy of the house being described as a single story, and the house next door having two stories, he explained that the new house had originally been constructed as a single-story home, but that the current owner had added the second story several years earlier. He described the current homeowner as being "a real nice guy," despite the oversized *No Trespassing* sign in his front window.

He went on to inform me that the woman who lived in the house had shared a gruesome story with him. He claimed that the woman had told him that she had dug up a partial human finger while planting flowers in her garden one day and that she had been "really grossed out" by the experience. He concluded by saying that was all he knew about Belle Gunness and his next-door neighbors. I inquired as to the possibility of conducting an after-hours paranormal investigation of his property if I were unable to secure permission from the current resident of Belle's property. The young man informed me that he didn't own the property and was only there to mow the grass. He further informed me that one of his relatives owned the property, but that this person wasn't home at the time. He suggested trying back at a later date if I couldn't get permission to perform an investigation from the next-door neighbor.

I thanked him for his time and returned to the van, where I filled my teammates in on what the young man had told me. I told them that I was still a bit apprehensive, but that I was going to walk up to Belle's old property and see if the current homeowner would be willing to speak with me. I felt it was a good idea for a single person to approach the homeowner rather than all four of us. As my teammates agreed, I exited the van for a second time and began the steep climb up the driveway that led to Belle's old stalking grounds. It was at that moment that the reality of what had taken place on the property nearly a century ago took hold in my imagination: a black vision of Belle's murderous romp filled my mind and enshrouded my spirit in its darkness. I had entered into the Blood Farm.

Of all Belle's suitors, only one survived to tell the tale of the men's ordeals at her farm. That suitor was Missourian George Anderson. As I climbed up the steep incline that led to the site of Belle's farmhouse, I imagined what it must have been like for George the night he made his fateful escape from Belle's sinister clutches.

One night during his stay at her farm, George had awakened in a cold sweat to find Belle standing over him, a flickering candle in her hand. The look on her face was so murderous that George jumped up in his bed and let out a cry. Without speaking a word, Belle ran from the room. George had been so frightened by the look on Belle's face that he fled the farm and ran all the way to La Porte, looking over his shoulder the entire way. George Anderson bought a ticket for the first available train back to Missouri and never even returned to the Gunness farm for his personal belongings.

As I walked up the hill, a sensation of foreboding washed over me as well. Was it just my subconscious playing tricks on me? Was the gruesome history of the property so powerful that it was overwhelming my senses? Or was the legacy of Belle's bloody reign imprinted so deeply in the land that even a century of time couldn't wash it away? It was a beautiful spring day, and the landscape was green and gorgeous, but even so, something about the property felt wrong. In terms of feelings and sensations, there is a darkness to Belle's former farm that cannot be understood unless it has been experienced firsthand. Shaking off my feeling of unease, I approached the back door of the house and rang the doorbell. No answer. Either no one was at home or the doorbell's ring was being ignored. I looked all around me, wondering if the ghosts of the past still lingered here. I snapped a few photographs and rejoined my teammates in the van.

The Kindly Neighbor

After repeated attempts over many weeks, I was finally able to contact the current homeowner. The news wasn't good. Even though the homeowner was open to the idea of WISP performing a paranormal investigation on his property, he told me that we would not be allowed to do so in the foreseeable future because he had recently signed a contract with a production company that was planning on filming a movie on his land based on the history of Belle Gunness. The contract gave the production company exclusive access to the property until their filming was completed.

I made the argument that what the production company was planning on filming was a *fictitious* account of the life and times of Belle Gunness, and what WISP wanted to do was to perform and record a *real-life* investigation. Unfortunately, my plea fell on deaf ears. For the time being at least, WISP would not be allowed on the property to investigate.

But the investigation wasn't dead in the water. At least not yet. As it turned out, the property right next door was for sale—property that was less than twenty-five feet away from Belle's former home. In Belle's time, the property she owned covered many acres of land. Today, that property is split into many smaller parcels. If the house was off limits, therefore, there were still quite a few options at our disposal. One way or another, I told myself, WISP would find a way to perform an investigation on the former property of Belle Gunness. As it turned out, getting permission to do so was as simple as walking right next door and ringing the doorbell.

The sign planted in the front yard of the house next door declared that the property was *For Sale by Owner*. This was good news for team WISP. It meant we wouldn't have to mess around with a real estate agent to get information about the property. It meant that we could go straight to the source.

Upon ringing the doorbell, I was greeted by an elderly gentleman who seemed more than happy to speak with me and tell me what he knew about his property and the history of Belle Gunness. The gentleman (whose name I will not disclose to protect his privacy) informed me that he had lived on the property for a very long time and that Belle's hog pen had once stood right in his backyard. This was the hog pen where many experts believe that Belle fed the remains of her victims to her hogs to dispose of the bodies.

The gentleman further informed me that over the years he had heard strange voices coming from the root cellar behind his house. He recounted quite a few instances when he would go down into the cellar (shotgun in hand) after hearing the voices, only to find that no one was there. *Well,* I recall thinking at the time, *at least no one that could be seen with the naked eye.* He also informed me that, on occasion, personal items in his home would be moved or go missing altogether.

After listening to the homeowner's tales of strange goings-on, I was convinced that strong and frequent paranormal activity was occurring on his property. But I still had to prove it. It was time to ask the $64,000 question: *would WISP be allowed on the property to investigate?* I was delighted to discover that the answer to this question was *yes.*

WISP was more than welcome to perform an investigation on the property. It was agreed with the homeowner that team WISP would be allowed access to the property at any time, provided we gave him twenty-four hours' notice. It was further agreed that a single member of the team would be allowed inside the cellar to investigate. WISP decided that the team member most qualified to perform the indoor investigation was me. Were the ghosts of the murderess Belle Gunness and her victims haunting these legendary grounds? We would soon find out.

In Search of the Ghost of Belle Gunness

Two weeks later, as WISP gathered our gear and prepared for the investigation, I admitted to my teammates that the thought of entering the cellar on my own was giving me an uneasy feeling. The thought of going below ground where so many of Belle's victims had been buried was unsettling, to say the least. There was also the question as to whether or not any of Belle's victims were still buried somewhere on the property. To date, only twelve bodies have been unearthed at the site of Belle's former home, but it is estimated that upwards of thirty undiscovered victims may still be buried there. Standing in the middle of a mass grave wasn't my idea of fun.

Then my subconscious started playing tricks on me. Try as I might to keep my thoughts from drifting into darkness, the visage of a spectral Belle Gunness standing in that shadowy cellar with a meat cleaver in her hands kept floating in my mind. If I did encounter the ghost of Belle Gunness, I wondered, would I be able to handle her alone? As abominable as Belle was in life, had her hellishness followed her to the grave? Locking away that horrible vision as best I could,

I popped fresh batteries into our digital audio recorders and helped my team load the rest of our gear into the van.

It was a crisp night in early May. As we drove toward La Porte and the ghosts of the past, the impending investigation occupied our thoughts. When we arrived at our destination, we found the homeowner waiting to greet us in the driveway. He informed us that he usually stayed up late to read, and we would have access to the property until around 11:30 p.m. He also reminded us that, as happy as he was to accommodate us, he preferred that only one member of the team enter the cellar. The reason he gave for this was because he had quite a bit of fishing gear stored there and that much of the gear was very old and possibly valuable. I informed him that I would do the honors myself and that his personal property would not be disturbed in any way.

As skeptical as the homeowner was about ghosts in general, though, he admitted that he was more than a little curious as to whether or not our research would provide hard evidence of paranormal activity occurring on his property. The homeowner then informed us that the door to the cellar was unlocked and that if we needed anything else, he would be inside the house, trying his best to stay out of our way.

It was at that point that the rest of the team and I went our separate ways. Although our usual modus operandi for an investigation would be to gather together in a circle and center our spirits, minds, and bodies, it had been decided beforehand that I should perform my own centering separately so as not to interfere with the rest of the team's energy signatures. In other words, we didn't want to establish an energy signature as a whole team and then potentially mess things up by going our separate ways. One of WISP's core beliefs is that otherworldly entities can pick up on human energy patterns in much the same way that a receiver picks up radio waves. In essence, if we were to establish an energy signature as a team and then split up, it would be the same as changing the channel on a radio to nothing but static. WISP wanted to give any ghosts prowling the area a clear signal to home in on.

Leaving the rest of the team behind me, I walked around to the back of the house and looked down into the cellar. I was well aware of the fact that less than thirty feet away from where I stood, the charred corpses of a headless female and Belle's three children—Myrtle, Lucy, and Phillip—had been discovered. WISP was on the scene of one of the grisliest crime scenes in American history.

I clicked on my flashlight and shone it down into the cellar. There were no electric lights down there and, judging by what little I could see, the cellar was very rustic and had a dirt floor. The team had brought video cameras along on the investigation, but I didn't bother taking one of them into the cellar with me. Our cameras were only equipped with infrared (IR) lighting installed at the factory, and stock IR lighting would be all but useless in such a dark space. Sam had been working on upgrading our camera's IR lights, but he still hadn't been able to design a portable power source that wasn't too heavy to carry comfortably. The rest of the team would have better luck with the cameras outdoors, where there was at least some natural lighting.

As I took the first step down into the cellar, I could feel my heart pounding in my chest. Standing still, I closed my eyes and cleared my mind. I centered my mind and spirit. I took in a deep, cleansing breath, then opened my eyes and continued down the stairs. The timeworn treads under my feet groaned and creaked. In the darkness above, the other members of the team were in search of unmarked graves.

The Ghosts of Memory

As I descended the stairs leading to the cellar, Sam, Becca, and Amber were searching for the most likely places to make contact with ghosts by using a tool and method that are highly unusual in modern times: they were using a divining rod (also known as a *witching rod*) to find the gravesites of Belle's undiscovered victims. Their divining rod was fashioned from a Y-forked tree branch they had harvested on-site. Once harvested, Sam, Becca, and Amber had used their magical skills to charge the divining rod and instill within it the desired intent. In this case, the intent was to locate the gravesites of Belle's victims.

A divining rod works by pulling (some diviners believe magnetically) the person holding it to the desired source. Once the source has been reached, it is not uncommon for the rod to vibrate gently in the user's hands, alerting the diviner that they have reached their destination. Becca had been drafted to be the first team member to give this fascinating tool a try, and within seconds of wielding it, she felt the sensation of being pulled. Trouble was, she was being pulled in many different directions at once, which led her to deduce that the remains of many of Belle's victims were still scattered around the property in unmarked graves.

Homing in on the strongest pull, Becca headed for the back edge of the property, the rest of the outdoor team right behind her. Sam and Amber used their digital audio recorders to ask the ghosts questions and gather EVP. Reaching the fence line at the back edge of the property, Becca continued to scan the area with her divining rod.

It was at that point that something quite remarkable and disturbing began to occur. Becca noticed that every time she felt a strong pull on her rod, a set of bamboo wind chimes hanging in a nearby tree began to rattle—a rattling that wasn't caused by the wind. There wasn't the slightest hint of a breeze blowing. As Becca, Sam, and Amber investigated this strange phenomenon and set up their video cameras, I was down in the cellar and the ghosts were making themselves known.

The Presence in the Cellar

There was a chill in the cellar that went far beyond anything I could blame on the coolness of the surrounding damp earth. It was a chill that creeps into a person's bones: the chill of being in the presence of something old, something not of our world. Finding my way to the back wall, I sat down in the corner, allowing myself only the light of the soft orange glow emanating from the faceplate of the digital audio recorder strapped to my arm. My senses were heightened by adrenaline, and I used them to my advantage. Every sound was alive, every smell intense and new. I settled myself in this dark, claustrophobic space and reached out with my mind. I softly spoke to the ghosts, letting them know that I meant them no harm and was only interested in making contact.

Within moments, the feeling of an unseen presence came from nowhere and slowly grew stronger and stronger. I was now at full attention. I cocked my head to the side and listened intently. I heard a shuffling sound, and then the soft patter of footsteps on the dirt floor.

Was there a living person in the cellar with me? It was unlikely. I certainly would have heard someone descending the creaky old stairs, and the homeowner had informed us that he had no children and that his wife had passed away many years earlier. Just to make sure, though, I clicked on my flashlight and scanned the cellar for any signs of life. Nothing. I clicked the light off. The shuffling sound resumed almost immediately. In breaks in the shuffling, I began hearing whispering. I couldn't make out what was being said, but the voice was decidedly male. Male and young.

"Phillip?" I asked, calling out to Belle's son, who had been found dead on the day that Ray Lamphere had burned the original house to the ground. "Is that you?" I asked.

There was no audible reply. I took another deep breath to keep myself centered, and the musky smells of earth and old wood filled my lungs. I could almost taste them settling on my tongue. I reached out with my senses and my third eye. Belle's former home, which was less than thirty feet away from where I now sat, felt empty and void, as though history itself had abandoned the horror of what had happened there a century earlier. But the cellar felt thick with the past. There was a youthful presence here. I could feel its innocence. As strange as it sounds, the presence felt playful.

I clicked on my flashlight again and looked around. That's when I noticed that an old pair of fishing waders that had been resting on the floor near the stairway had been moved. I know for a fact that they were moved, because I had nearly tripped over them while making my descent into the cellar. I had made a mental note of where they were resting so I wouldn't trip over them on my way out.

I stood up and was about to investigate the waders when I started to hear a rattling sound coming from the opposite end of the cellar. Shining my flashlight into the far corner of the room, I saw a vertical rack lined with old fishing poles and tackle. Three of the fishing poles were vibrating as though caught in an earthquake. The vibrating continued for well over thirty seconds; then, as I watched, one by one every fishing pole in the rack sat up straight, then toppled to the floor. Now I heard the giggling of a child. There was a poltergeist in the cellar with me. I was certain of it.

The poltergeist activity also explained the strange goings-on that the homeowner had told me about. It is well known that poltergeists like to move and steal objects in a playful manner. Poltergeists are also known to be more annoying than harmful, so for the moment I was more intrigued than frightened by the activity in the cellar. But all that was about to change.

From out of nowhere, a powerful odor suddenly washed through the cellar. It was the unmistakable odor of rot and death. The first time I had ever smelled the scent of death was during a visit to the hospital when I was a very young boy, perhaps no more than six or seven years old. My grandmother had taken my sister and me with her to the hospital after my aunt Josie died. My grandmother left my sister and me in the hospital room with the body while she went to have a conversation with Josie's doctor. That day the smell of death left its indelible mark on my memory.

The odor in the cellar was very similar to what we had smelled in the hospital room. But here it was much, much stronger. It was so intense, in fact, that it made my eyes water and my nostrils sting. That horrid smell filled my throat, nearly gagging me. I quickly walked over to the stairs. My stomach was starting to churn, and I was certain that if I didn't leave the cellar immediately, I was going to be sick. As I moved toward the stairs, my flashlight beam showed a darkness even blacker than the shadows. The darkness grew larger. It flooded over the wall. As it did this, I sensed the childlike presence in the cellar cowering. Whatever the darkness was, the poltergeist was obviously frightened of it. *Should I be frightened, too?* I asked myself.

As I pondered this question, the darkness slowly moved toward me. With it came the smell of death. Without the support of my team, I knew it was time for me to get out. Whatever was stalking the cellar was powerful and not of our world. My safety was in jeopardy.

As I reached the staircase I cautiously placed a foot on the first tread and started climbing. About halfway up the staircase, I felt something hit me hard in the middle of my back. Something powerful. It knocked the wind out of me. My legs buckled. I fell forward, and my right knee went down hard on one of the treads. I cried out in pain. My flashlight and digital audio recorder fell from my hands and landed on the dirt floor behind the stairs.

The Intermingling
of Past and Present

Outside in the yard, Sam, Becca, and Amber had made an interesting discovery. Sam had been following Becca with an electromagnetic field (EMF) detector as the divining rod pulled her around the property. He noticed that every time Becca felt a pull on the rod, his EMF detector registered the presence of a strong EMF close by.

Many ghost hunters, amateur and professional alike, believe that the presence of an EMF that cannot be associated with a source of electricity, such as a power line or a lamp, signals the presence of a non-biological entity (NBE). Even though the EMF detector is an interesting tool, the members of WISP are in some disagreement as to whether or not an EMF actually signals the presence of a ghost. WISP believes that electromagnetic fields are only one small part of the paranormal puzzle, and Sam has recently been hard at work designing a multi-field detector capable of registering not only EMFs but also atmospheric vibration, air density, temperature, and ultra-broadband fields using an array of electro-optic sensors.

Nevertheless, the team was wondering if Sam's EMF detector and Becca's divining rod were both registering the ghosts of Belle Gunness's victims. As Becca pointed out to Sam and Amber where the pull on her divining rod was the strongest, my teammates deduced that they must be very close to the part of the property where Belle's hog pen is believed to have once stood. Many Gunness experts believe that she fed the severed limbs of some of her victims to her hogs to help dispose of the bodies. The former site of the hog pen thus seemed a likely place to find the ghosts of Belle's victims.

As the outdoor team investigated the hog pen, I was alone down in the cellar and engaged in battle with an entity that was not of our world.

Alone in the Dark

I was determined to retrieve my flashlight and digital recorder. The only problem was getting to them behind the stairs. Whatever was in the cellar with me was obviously angry and capable of manifesting an intense amount of physical force on the earthly plane.

I was all alone in the dark with a malevolent entity. The smells of rot and death had gotten even worse. Only a minute earlier, I would have sworn this was impossible, but it was getting very difficult to breathe. I didn't have much time. I either had to leave the cellar or fight back. I'd had enough of being bullied by ghosts. My hand fell upon the handle of my ritual knife. The knife, which isn't meant to cut anything on the physical plane, was the one metaphysical tool that I made sure to have on me at all times during our investigations. It was very old and charged with great power. I had used it successfully many times in the past to ward off troublesome spirits, but I had never before used it to face down a force as powerful as the one that was with me now. Would a mere knife work against such a force? I didn't know, but I was willing to give it a try.

Fumbling only once with my shaking hand, I managed to unsheathe the blade from its leather holster. I held the knife before me, waving it from side to side through the darkness.

With the first wave, I could feel the unseen force back away from me, if only just a little. "Leave now," I said in a firm voice, daring the presence to face my own power, "or I will do everything I can to fight you."

At that moment I felt a flux in the energy pattern coming from the unseen presence. The presence moved toward me again, as if daring me, then retreated deeper into the cellar. I felt this flux several more times. I slowly took a step down the stairs, brandishing the knife before me, pushing with its power. I felt the presence move even deeper into the recesses of the cellar. Soon I could no longer feel the entity's presence.

Reaching the bottom of the stairs, I got behind them and went down on my hands and knees to search the floor with my free hand. I retrieved my flashlight, clicked it on, and scanned the cellar. Nothing. Even the horrid smell had begun to fade away. But I knew I still wasn't safe. Not all alone in the cellar without the rest of my team, anyway.

I shone the flashlight down at my feet and saw my recorder. I quickly snatched it up from the dirt and stuffed it into my pocket. Taking one last look around, I was satisfied that I had been successful in chasing the unseen entity away, if only for the moment, but I knew that a force as powerful as this one could easily return if it wanted to. I ran up the stairs and went in search of the rest if my team.

Convergence

They were still near the back edge of the property. Rejoining them, I discovered that as they came near Belle's hog pen, they had experienced the same smells of rot and death that I had smelled down in the cellar. Being outside in the open air, however, they were able to tolerate it for much longer than I could.

I learned that they had also felt a powerful unseen presence in their midst, but, unlike me, none of them had been physically touched by the presence. Scanning the hog pen with his EMF detector and a digital IR thermometer, Sam had located multiple pockets of cold just below the surface of the ground, a few of which registered well below 30 degrees Fahrenheit. Interestingly, he had been able to locate the pockets by scanning the area of land where Becca had been pulled by her divining rod. Both Sam and Becca had been able to register these areas using very different tools. But there was no earthly explanation for these pockets of cold. To team WISP, they possibly signaled the presence of ghosts and/or vortices leading to or from the otherworld.

After hearing what I had experienced down in the cellar, my teammates suggested that I talk to the homeowner to see if he would allow Sam and his equipment to accompany me back down there. The team wanted to know if similar pockets of cold were also present in the cellar. Becca and Amber said that they would be just fine on their own and that they had some metaphysical and scientific experiments they wanted to conduct at the site of the hog pen. I agreed that speaking with the homeowner was a good idea and informed my team that I had to tell him about his disheveled fishing gear, anyway. Even though ghosts (not me!) had toppled the gear, it was WISP's investigation, and we were responsible for making restitution for any damages.

Unfortunately, however, before Sam and I could speak with the homeowner, Mother Nature intervened with a vengeance. As we stood at the edge of the hog pen where Belle had committed her gruesome crimes, the air became thick with the sound of crickets and the smell of coming rain. We could see tremendous black storm clouds billowing in the night sky. Soon the wind picked up, and the sky flashed and crackled with the sights and sounds of thunder and lightning. We knew that we had to get our cameras and other gear stowed inside the van immediately or risk losing our valuable equipment. Moving as fast as we could, we scurried around the property collecting our gear. We managed to get everything stowed in the van just as the rain began hammering down.

With the team and the gear safely inside the van, I ran to the house and knocked on the front door. The homeowner greeted me with a grin.

"I see you got a little damp there, son," he said.

I returned his grin and agreed that things had gotten a little wet over the last fifteen minutes. Never once mentioning the ghosts, I told him about what had happened to his fishing gear and said I would be more than happy to pay for any damages. He assured me that it wasn't the first time he had gone down into the cellar to find his gear in disarray. He said he was sure his fishing gear would be "just fine." I thanked him for his kindness and hospitality, told him that I would let him know if we turned up any evidence of paranormal activity occurring on his property, then turned away and hurried back to the van.

After I rejoined my teammates inside the van, we all expressed our delight in what we had experienced and our dismay at the investigation ending so abruptly.

But the investigation of Belle Gunness and her horrible crimes was far from over. Less than four miles from where we sat was the cemetery where many of Belle's victims were buried, not least of which was her last known victim, Andrew Helgelien.

Investigating the cemetery, now called Patton Cemetery, was our next logical step. Even though it was possible that WISP might be allowed to return to Belle's former property at a later date, for the time being we would have to pursue other options. With minds full of wonder at the things we had experienced during our investigation of the former home of Belle Gunness, we drove back to base and began sifting through the evidence.

The Evidence

Photographic evidence: No conclusive evidence of paranormal activity was captured on camera or camcorder during our investigation. However, WISP was able to use an IR thermometer to document the pockets of cold where Belle's hog pen once stood as evidence of paranormal activity.

Audio evidence: Multiple EVP were recorded during the investigation. However, many of the EVP we collected were very poor in quality and therefore cannot be documented as being paranormal in origin. What follows are descriptions of the EVP that were of high enough quality to be submitted as evidence.

Belle Gunness EVP in Chronological Order of their Capture

1. After the investigator asks, "Phillip? Is that you?" a young, disembodied male voice repeats the name "Phillip," and then continues by saying, "Let's play." These EVP were captured down in the cellar.

2. The giggling of a young, male poltergeist was captured on digital audio recorder, followed by the disembodied voice of an angry, adult female that snarls, "Leave now!" These EVP were recorded seconds before the unseen presence hit me in the back on my way up the stairs and knocked the equipment out of my hands. These EVP were also captured down in the cellar.

3. A number of wailing voices were captured on audio recorder near the site of Belle's hog pen. The wailing is reminiscent of a large number of people in simultaneous mourning, similar to what a person would expect to hear during a funeral.

4. A single, anomalous male voice was captured near the hog pen that declares, "All dead here. All dead."

Conclusion

The investigation of the Belle Gunness property was an intriguing glimpse into the world of the paranormal. Team WISP would like to send out another round of thanks to the homeowner (wherever he may be) for his hospitality and for allowing us onto his property to investigate such a bloody and brutal slice of American history. Although WISP members had personal paranormal experiences during the investigation, me in particular, there is no hard scientific data to back them up and therefore they cannot be submitted as evidence. However, combined with the hard evidence that we *were* able to collect, WISP was able to document that the personal experiences coincided precisely with the paranormal activity occurring on the Gunness property during the investigation. The evidence and our experiences back each other up.

On a personal note, I will tell you that the presence that attacked me down in the cellar was without a doubt the darkest and most powerful otherworldly entity I have ever encountered. The sheer physical force that the entity was able to manifest on the earthly plane was mind-numbing in its power and implications. In my opinion, such a force can only be born from evil, the kind of evil that Belle Gunness wielded with such heartless precision during her bloody reign in La Porte, Indiana, in the early years of the twentieth century.

Chapter 2

Rumley Road: Patton Cemetery and the Victims of the Gunness Horror

Investigation: Patton Cemetery

Start date: July 13, 2006

Place: La Porte, Indiana

Research and Discovery[3]

With the paranormal investigation of the murderess Belle Gunness complete, next on WISP's agenda was to plan the investigation of Patton Cemetery, where we would attempt to make contact with the ghosts of some of Belle's known victims. Andrew Helgelien and Jennie Olson (Belle's foster daughter), both of whom had been victims of the Blood Farm Horror, were interred in Patton Cemetery. Peter Gunness, Belle's second husband (who many believe Belle murdered by bashing him in the head with a meat grinder), is also said to be interred within Patton's hallowed grounds.

WISP decided to first pay a daytime visit to Patton Cemetery to survey the lay of the land and locate the graves

---

3. The Patton Cemetery page on the Cemetery and Research Association of La Porte County, Indiana, website (www.dunelady.com/laporte/ cemeteries/patton/patton.htm), updated by D. West with information from Patricia Gruse Harris, was a source of historical background for this chapter.

of Helgelien, Olson, and Peter Gunness. As we drove past McClung Road on our way to Patton, two members of the team expressed concerns about the paranormal aspect of the Patton Cemetery investigation, about attempting to make contact with the ghosts of murder victims. After some discussion, though, we agreed that the investigation was too intriguing to abandon and that we would be able to handle any encounters with troublesome spirits.

When approaching Patton Cemetery during the day, the first thing one notices is the bizarre visual phenomenon created by two rows of large pine trees that line the entrance. From two blocks away, the entrance to Patton Cemetery looks like a huge black vortex waiting to suck in any unsuspecting passersby. The second thing one notices about Patton Cemetery is that it's massive. Locating the graves of Jennie Olson, Peter Gunness, and Andrew Helgelien was going to be a chore.

The layout of Patton Cemetery is confusing at best. (I've read reports of paranormal investigators getting lost trying to find their way out of Patton after nightfall.) There are nineteen or more separate burial sections, many of which carry names like the Garden of Meditation, the Garden of Memories, the Garden of Devotion, and the Garden of Blessings. According to an online burial listing, Jennie Olson and Andrew Helgelien were buried in graves 8 and 9 of what is called the tier section, but even with a detailed map it took us more than thirty minutes to locate the tier section and another fifteen minutes to locate the graves. Andrew Helgelien's grave looked like it had been vandalized. His headstone had been toppled to the ground.

The Grave of Andrew Helgelien

At the time of team WISP's initial visit, there were an unusually high number of toppled headstones at Patton Cemetery. Upon seeing the damage, I recalled reading an article on the Internet that mentioned a local legend about toppling a specific headstone in Patton Cemetery. The legend suggested that toppling the correct headstone would entice the grave's resident ghost to appear and give chase, which made me wonder if there wasn't a connection between this legend and the large number of vandalized graves. Andrew's headstone was lying flat on the ground, and, fortunately for us, the inscription was facing up. If the inscription had been facing down, we probably would have never located the grave. The inscription on Andrew's headstone is chilling.

> *Andrew K. Helgelien*
> *1859–1908*
> *The Last Victim of the*
> *Gunness Horror*
> *Remains Found by His Brother*
> *Asle K. Helgelien*
> *May 8, 1908*
> *Rest In Peace*

My first instinct was to right Andrew's headstone, but the headstone proved to be too heavy to be lifted by hand. Unable to return the headstone to its foundation, I knelt on the ground next to it, closed my eyes, and placed my hand on the grave. I imagined what Andrew's last night on earth might have been like, a night spent in the company of a heartless murderer. I wondered if he had known he was going to die, or if the fatal blow had come without warning. I couldn't help but wonder if Belle Gunness had taken pleasure in taunting her victims before murdering them.

According to our burial listing, the graves of Jennie Olson and Peter Gunness were located right next to Andrew's. But none of the graves adjacent to Andrew's seemed to belong to Jennie Olson or Peter Gunness. There were several headstones in the tier section with unintelligible inscriptions, but none of them were anywhere near the grave of Andrew Helgelien. Either the burial listing was wrong, or the headstones were missing.

I suggested to my teammates that it was possible that Jennie might be buried next to Andrew but was never given a grave marker. Jennie Olson was Belle's adopted daughter, and, with Belle dead or missing, Jennie was most likely buried by the state of Indiana with little ceremony and even less money, a sad ending indeed for the victim of such a grisly crime. The missing grave of Peter Gunness was a mystery, but through burial records we deduced that the grave of Peter Gunness had to be in the immediate vicinity of the grave of Andrew Helgelien.

In April of 2008, the graves of Jennie Olson and Peter Gunness were marked with headstones for the first time in over a century. As WISP suspected, their graves were located adjacent to the grave of Andrew Helgelien. A headstone was also erected in memoriam of the unidentified victims of the Gunness murders.

Next on our agenda was to scope out the rest of the cemetery so we wouldn't lose our bearings after nightfall. Patton's semicircular layout allowed us to pinpoint key areas and mark them on our map. We soon felt confident in our ability to navigate Patton Cemetery in the dark.

After snapping a few more photographs, we left Patton and returned to our base of operations to prepare for our nighttime incursion. I had already secured permission from the La Porte Police Department to enter Patton Cemetery after hours, so all that was left to do was ready our minds, spirits, and equipment, and wait for darkness to fall. To my knowledge, there had been a small number of previous paranormal investigations performed at Patton Cemetery, but none had produced any compelling evidence of otherworldly activity. Were we wasting our time? Or would our presence entice the spirits of Patton Cemetery to come out and play?

Patton Cemetery after Dark

An unspoken excitement was chasing through us as we readied our equipment and prepared for our nighttime investigation. My gut instinct told me that we would find compelling evidence of paranormal activity. I was eager to get the mission underway. WISP had recently acquired two new digital camcorders that incorporate infrared technology. Tonight would be our first field test. We had also recently developed several new metaphysical techniques for paranormal investigation and would be trying them out tonight.

After a final check of the equipment, team WISP piled into the van and headed for La Porte and the ghosts of Patton Cemetery. As we drove toward our destination, fireworks displays lit up the horizon. It was nearly the end of July, but the celebratory illuminations this year showed no signs of ending.

About twenty minutes into the drive, we discovered that we had acquired a new team member. There was a ghostly presence in the van. Becca felt a pair of unseen hands brush over her face and down the back of her hair, then Sam felt something brush against him. Someone we couldn't see had apparently hitched a ride with us at my home, which is our base of operations. Becca and Amber were excited about this paranormal tag-along. "What a unique opportunity we have when an active spirit joins us on an investigation," Becca said.

But I wasn't so enthused. Unique opportunity or not, allowing the spirit to accompany us meant only one thing to me: contamination of the investigation. If we allowed the spirit to remain in our presence, I said, when we examined the evidence, there would be no way to discern between paranormal activity indigenous to Patton Cemetery and activity generated by the spirit we'd brought along with us. Evidence collected at Patton Cemetery would be useless.

I asked Becca and Amber to exorcise the spirit, but Amber made an interesting proposition. Why not contain the spirit in the van instead of expelling it? "Having the spirit in our presence," she argued, "gives us a rare opportunity for scientific and metaphysical study." She wanted to see if and how the spirit would react to the investigation.

I reluctantly agreed, but after long debate on the subject, we decided to put the kibosh on containment. Trying to imprison an entity we knew nothing about was a bad idea. What would it do to the inside of my van?

As we neared La Porte, flashes of light once again lit up the skyline, but this time the flashes were lightning. A storm was brewing, and there was nothing we could do. Our investigation was looking like a wash in more ways than one. I was considering turning the van around and calling it a night, but my teammates coaxed me to press on. We were still several miles from the cemetery, and they were confident that the storm would blow over by the time we arrived. As it turned out, they were right.

Although it had been raining heavily in downtown La Porte, by the time we reached Patton Cemetery the storm had subsided to a light drizzle. There were breaks in the clouds, and the sight of twinkling stars filled us with hope. I navigated the van to the tier section and parked near the grave of Andrew Helgelien.

It was at that point that our ghostly hitchhiker made itself known to me. Not long after I killed the engine, I started hearing whispering. I turned on the interior lights and queried my teammates. "Who's whispering?" I asked. "Have any of you guys heard a voice?" Their answer to both questions was no. I asked Becca to dig my digital recorder out of the equipment bag so I could capture the voice on audio. I also instructed my teammates to begin prepping their equipment. After recording a decent amount of audio inside the van, we got out and walked the short distance to Andrew's grave.

Our nighttime investigation of Patton Cemetery was officially underway.

A Grave Adventure

As team WISP approached the grave of Andrew Helgelien, we noticed something new: an urn of fresh flowers had been placed before his headstone, which was still lying flat on the ground. Andrew had come to La Porte from South Dakota to stay with Belle, and to our knowledge he has no descendants living in northern Indiana. Who left the flowers?

Our first order of business was to try to initiate contact with Andrew's spirit (assuming he was prowling the cemetery grounds at all) by using our occult skills. For a second time, I knelt next to Andrew's grave and placed my hand on his headstone. The headstone was quite warm, and I stated so to my teammates. Sam took a reading of Andrew's headstone with his digital thermometer. It registered a warm eighty-two degrees.

It was at that moment that I caught movement out of the corner of my eye. Turning my head for a better look, I saw a soft glow of light about the size of a golf ball hovering a few inches above the ground, three feet away from Andrew's grave. I observed the ball of light for a moment, then reached for it, but as I did the light faded and vanished.

Was the ball of light paranormal in origin? None of the equipment we were using at the time was capable of producing the phenomenon. Unable to conjure a natural explanation for the ball of light, I once again turned my attention to Andrew's grave. I placed my hand on the headstone for a second time, and the unmistakable prickle of gooseflesh ran up my arm. Andrew's headstone, which had been quite warm only a few moments earlier, was now ice-cold.

I asked Sam to take a second reading with his digital thermometer. The temperature of the headstone was now registering at sixty-three degrees. I asked my teammates to place their hands on Andrew's headstone next to mine. We pictured Andrew as clearly as we could in our minds and spoke to him in calm, soothing voices. Amber told him that we had only come to his grave to make contact. "We mean you no harm," I added.

When Becca said, "He was only looking for love," I couldn't help myself. I just had to say it: "…in all the wrong places." Our somber mood dissolved into laughter. I hoped that Andrew had a good sense of humor when he was alive and that he'd taken it with him to the grave.

Our next step was to raise energy in hopes of thinning the veil between the worlds of the living and the dead and luring the ghosts of Patton Cemetery out of hiding. To do this, we stood in a circle around Andrew's grave, grasped hands, and focused on our intent to make contact. We focused on open communication with the resident spirits and the team's ability to see clearly beyond our world.

WISP's method for raising energy differs from the typical methods used by garden-variety occult practitioners. Whereas many occult groups raise energy by chanting, drumming, or dancing in a circle, WISP raises energy by building the energy internally as individuals, then passing the energy to the next team member in the circle where it is further enhanced before being released. In other words, each member of WISP focuses on the goal and intent of the energy to be raised, and builds the energy within himself or herself, and then, with the individually raised energy at its height, passes the energy to the next person via willpower and a squeeze of the hand as a trigger.

Once that person has received the energy, his or her own energy is added to it before it is passed to the next person in the circle. This process is continued at an ever-growing pace (envision a nuclear accelerator), until the desired energy has been raised. Once the group energy is at its height, it is released to do its job.

Once the job of raising and sending energy was accomplished, we set off for the heart of Patton Cemetery. We were after its resident spirits. It didn't take us long to find them. We had no sooner passed the first row of graves that make up the center section of Patton Cemetery than Becca saw someone (or some*thing*) walking between two headstones a few yards ahead of her. She also heard a voice. Clicking on her flashlight, she ran to the graves to investigate, but whatever she had seen was gone. We searched the surrounding area thoroughly but found nothing.

That's when I happened to look up at the night sky. "Oh, look," I said, "the Big Dipper."

And now the ghosts of Patton Cemetery began to speak…

Voices in the Night

The minute I commented on the stars, I stared hearing whispers somewhere close behind me. Still searching for whatever was moving around in the cemetery, the rest of the team had already ventured beyond the first few rows of graves and were a good thirty yards away, so I was reasonably certain that it wasn't their voices I was hearing. As I walked back toward my teammates, the voices seemed to follow me. I stopped walking and asked the spirits for a sign of their presence. They responded. I heard the muffled thump of something hitting the ground at my feet. I clicked on my flashlight for a better look at the surrounding area. As I did, an unseen presence brushed up against my shoulder with enough force to knock me off balance.

Righting myself, I now heard what sounded like heavy, wet clothing being dragged across the ground. The sound was moving in the direction of my teammates. I stood completely still for a moment and listened. Nothing more. The activity had apparently moved away from where I was standing. I quickly made my way to my teammates and wasn't at all surprised to hear Becca telling Sam and Amber that she had heard what sounded like a heavy robe being dragged across the ground. I shared what I had experienced with the team and told them to be prepared for anything. If the dead wanted to play, we were game.

I made note of our experiences on my audio recorder and led the team deep into the oldest section of Patton Cemetery.

WISP spent the next few hours investigating the four sections that make up the center of Patton's funerary grounds. These sections are Lake View, the Plains, and Plum Tree Grove, along with the semicircular Wayside Retreat at the heart of Patton Cemetery. Other than the voices, the possible apparition Becca had witnessed on the outskirts of the cemetery, and our earlier personal experiences, the team had little else to report. Becca and Amber had come across several graves that gave them a tingle in the pit of the stomach when they stood near them, but nothing more.

The older sections of Patton Cemetery now offered little else in the way of otherworldly feelings or sensations. The spooky trees and century-old monuments towering overhead were interesting to look at and stimulated our imaginations, but we sensed nothing supernatural lurking within their shadows. I commented that perhaps the ghosts in this part of the cemetery were "too old and crusty to make further contact" and suggested that we might have better luck in one of Patton's newer sections. My teammates agreed, so we packed up our equipment and headed for the van. Unbeknownst to us, things were about to get interesting.

Gardens of the Dead

Even after dark, distinguishing the newer sections of Patton Cemetery from the older sections was simplicity itself. While the older sections are a snarl of trees, graves, statuary, and dirt pathways, the garden sections, which hold the newer gravesites, are open fields with modern headstones surrounded by paved roadways. When we entered the Garden of Devotion, the investigation took a turn toward the eerie.

We all felt, though we didn't say aloud, that the garden sections felt different from the older sections, and not in a way that was comforting. The air felt heavier, the shadows more menacing. Solar-powered crosses dotted the fields, and their light washed the headstones in an eerie blue glow. And there seemed to be a looming presence here. Instead of individually dispersing throughout the graveyard as is typical of our investigations, we felt compelled to roam the gardens in pairs. Making sure to stay within earshot of the rest of the team, Becca and I headed into the Garden of Meditation to shoot some video, while Sam and Amber patrolled the outskirts of the nearby Garden of Memories. We didn't remain separated for long.

No sooner had Becca begun filming than I started catching movement out of the corners of my eyes. I remained calm and quietly pointed out likely places for her to shoot, but every time I would direct her, the movement would stop there and start up somewhere else. It seemed as though whatever was moving among the headstones was aware of the camera and was toying with us. I was about to suggest that we mount the camera on a tripod and let it run unattended for a while when Amber called out to us.

Domesticated Spectral Entities?

Sam and Amber were hunting cats, not just ghosts. They had repeatedly heard a cat meowing somewhere nearby, but were unable to locate it, and so I made the halfhearted suggestion that maybe it was a ghost cat. Amber and I set off in search of spectral critters. After several minutes, Becca and Sam rejoined us, and they didn't look very happy. Becca informed us that she and Sam had heard a loud growl directly behind them, but when they turned, nothing was there. At least nothing that could be seen with the naked eye. Even our resident skeptic, Sam, said it was the most unearthly sound he had ever heard. "Whatever growled at us," he said, "it's sure not of this world." The look on his face as he spoke was enough to give me goose bumps.

Although neither Amber nor I heard the growl, I've heard otherworldly growling in the past, and I can tell you from experience that it's fairly unsettling. I don't personally believe in the existence of demonic entities in the satanic sense, but I've seen enough to know that not everything prowling the netherworld is friendly or good-intentioned. There are entities lurking in other worlds we should be cautious of.

We were unable to locate a cat, spectral or otherwise. It was getting very late, and we were starting to talk about wrapping up and heading for home. It was an hour and a half drive back to our base of operations, and we had many hours of audio and video to examine, not to mention hundreds of digital photographs. I was about to instruct the team to pack up their gear when the dead began to speak again.

Becca and Amber were leaning over a grave, smelling a basket of fresh flowers, when they started hearing the voices. Then Sam and I heard the voices. The four of us stood in silence, listening to the sounds of the night. Were the dead really speaking? The answer was *yes*.

Although faint, the voices were close—*very* close. There was no doubt in our minds that the voices were paranormal in origin. We slowly prowled the gardens of the dead, asking the ghosts questions and attempting to record their voices. We soon came upon several fresh graves, and as Amber read the name *Robert Boardman* aloud from one of the headstones, something spoke the name back. Suddenly, I heard a faint growl and the meow of a cat. The growl and the meow were unlike any earthly sound I had ever heard.

We're attracting too much attention, I thought to myself. *We're drawing in too many questionable entities*. I was starting to worry about the team's safety. Although I felt confident in our ability to fend off any troublesome spirits, whatever was growling at us felt dark and angry. It felt as though we were being stalked. I was ready to suggest that it might be a good idea to cast a protective circle when all at once the air seemed to lighten and we could no longer sense the presence of unseen entities. Had the entities picked up on our intentions and fled?

One of the most popular theories about ghosts is that they must draw upon a source of energy other than their own to be able to manifest and/or communicate verbally. When WISP goes into protective mode, our energy patterns change drastically, and even though we hadn't actually cast a protective circle, it seems to me that the subtle changes in our energy patterns alone might have been enough to repel the ghosts of Patton Cemetery. No longer sensing any unusual activity in the gardens of the dead, we retreated to the van and made the long drive home, wondering at what we had experienced during the investigation. Even our ghostly hitchhiker had vanished without a trace.

When we started sifting through the evidence, we were overwhelmed by what we had captured during the investigation. Our audio recordings were littered with the voices of the dead.

The Evidence

Photographic evidence: No conclusive evidence of paranormal activity was captured on camera or camcorder during our investigation of Patton Cemetery. An anomalous "orb" was captured on camera during our daytime investigation, but WISP has concluded that the anomaly is probably a rare form of lens flare.

Audio evidence: Multiple EVP were captured on audio recorders during our nighttime investigation of Patton Cemetery.

Patton Cemetery EVP in Chronological Order of Their Capture

1. Disembodied voice: A male voice is captured inside the WISP van that says, "Strange power." At the time this voice is captured, team WISP is preparing electronic equipment for the investigation.

2. Disembodied voice: Immediately after team WISP exits the van, an animal-like voice is captured that says, "You need to go home."

3. Disembodied voice: A female voice is captured in the tier section of Patton Cemetery saying, "Turn the lights off." Comparing the audio evidence to the video evidence, we discover that the voice is also captured on camcorder, and that at the time of capture all four members of the team have their flashlights trained on a single headstone.

4. Investigator: "Tell us your name." Disembodied voice: "Claire."

5. Investigator: "Oh look, the Big Dipper." Disembodied male voice: "Shhh! Big Dipper." Approximately fifteen seconds of time elapses between the investigator's comment about the Big Dipper and the disembodied voice's response, eliminating the possibility of the voice being an echo. This EVP does not mimic the investigator word for word.

6. Disembodied voices: A male voice says, "Body back there." A female voice responds, "I know." The male voice sounds remarkably similar to the Big Dipper

EVP. The female voice sounds desperate and other-worldly.

7. Disembodied voice: "We have questions." At the time this voice is captured, WISP is discussing possible metaphysical techniques to be used during the investigation.

8. Investigator: "Boy, he married 'em young." The investigator is commenting on an inscription on an older gentleman's headstone listing his three teenage wives. Disembodied voices: A male voice says, "Shh!" followed by a female voice saying, "I'll never learn." WISP is, in fact, shushed quite often during the investigation of Patton Cemetery.

9. Investigator (speaking to a fellow investigator): "Hi, back there." Disembodied voices: A male voice immediately says, "Fresh grave," followed by a female voice that mimics the investigator by repeating, "Hi, back there" four times. Interestingly, approximately five minutes after these EVP are captured, team WISP discovers a fresh grave.

10. Disembodied voice: A loud moan is captured, followed by an eerie female voice that says, "I scared them."

11. Disembodied voice: This EVP isn't a voice, but the otherworldly growl that Becca and Sam heard in the Garden of Memories. Without question this growl is the most chilling EVP I have ever heard. I would stake my reputation as an author and an investigator

that whatever growled at Becca and Sam in the Garden of Memories is not from our plane of existence.

12. Disembodied voices: After a female voice asks, "Do you need your cat?" a male voice says, "Talking, they're talking." The female voice is an A-class EVP and is the clearest and loudest voice WISP has captured to date. It is also one of the strangest EVP that WISP has captured. The voice was recorded approximately fifteen minutes after Amber and Sam heard the cat meowing and clearly demonstrates that the female entity was aware of us and the events of our investigation.

13. Investigator: "Is there anyone here that would like to say something to us?" Disembodied female voice: "They are near our headstone now."

14. Female investigator reads the name "Robert Boardman" aloud from a headstone. A disembodied male voice repeats the name "Robert Boardman."

Conclusion

At the time of our investigation, Patton Cemetery was a hotbed of paranormal activity and produced the most compelling audio evidence of ghostly entities team WISP has captured to date. The sheer number of active EVP recorded during the investigation was overwhelming. Of all the voices captured, however, there is no evidence to suggest that any of them belonged to the ghosts of Jennie Olson, Peter Gunness, or Andrew Helgelien. Whether or not the spirits of Belle's victims prowl the grounds of Patton Cemetery remains unconfirmed. WISP was fascinated by the fact that most of the audio evidence was collected in the newer sections of Patton Cemetery rather than the older sections. This is contrary to the evidence we have collected during previous cemetery investigations, where little or no evidence of paranormal activity was gathered around newer graves. The EVP captured inside the van seems to verify the presence of the ghostly hitchhiker, although the entity's point of origin cannot be confirmed. Whether or not the entity was indigenous to Patton Cemetery is unknown.

WISP's ability to collect compelling evidence of paranormal activity has increased exponentially over the last few years, and begs the question *why*? I theorize that as a collective team, we are a natural magnet for paranormal activity and that, as our skills increase, so does our ability to attract and detect otherworldly entities. I theorize that the combination of WISP's four core members is a rare and perfect mix of energy patterns that fosters natural paranormal activity. Little did I know, however, that over the next several months I would get the chance to put my theories to the test.

Several weeks after the investigation of Patton Cemetery, Sam and Amber made the life-changing decision to sell their home in Rockford, Illinois, and move to northern Indiana. This was good news for the team, but the move would be a massive undertaking and would separate us for a time.

If any investigations were going to take place over the summer months, therefore, Becca and I would have to conduct them on our own. It didn't take long for us to become antsy. I started looking into other prospective locations for Becca and me to investigate over the summer. I came up with several strong possibilities, but I had yet to do preliminary research into the backgrounds of the cases and secure permission to investigate them. We were both eager to get back into the game, so we decided to return to Patton Cemetery on our own. Would the ghosts come out to play for just the two of us?

The Return to Patton Cemetery: Do You Need Your Cat?

After calling the night officer at the La Porte City Police Department and informing him of our intention to further our investigation, Becca and I packed our gear and headed back to Patton Cemetery. We arrived without incident, but much to our dismay we discovered that the neighbors who live along the outskirts of the eastern edge of the cemetery were having a block party, complete with a live band and fireworks. Collecting untainted audio evidence was going to be impossible. Becca suggested that we go ahead and drive to the part of the cemetery that was farthest from the activity and shoot some video. She reminded me that the Jewish burial plots (the only section of Patton we hadn't previously investigated) were located in the far end of the cemetery, and would be interesting to check out. I agreed and maneuvered the van onto one of Patton's paved roads. We began a slow drive through the burial ground.

As we neared the Jewish section, at the far end of the Garden of Memories, something unusual appeared in the van's headlights. A young woman was standing just off the edge of the road directly ahead of us and cradling a black cat in her arms. As we drove nearer, I noticed that a white cat was sitting on the ground at her feet. Interested in why a woman was standing all alone in the middle of a graveyard late at night with two cats, I pulled the van alongside her and rolled down my window. "Did your kitties get out?" I asked her. The woman just stared at me. Something about the look on her face sent a chill over me. It was obvious that my question was unwelcome. I slowly pulled away, but kept watch on the woman in the van's driver's side mirror. She didn't appear to be going anywhere.

I hadn't driven more than fifteen feet when realization dawned in me. I looked over at Becca. Her eyes were as big as full moons. She had come to the same conclusion—the woman was standing in almost the exact spot where we had recorded the EVP that asked, *Do you need your cat?* I slammed on the brakes and looked in the mirror. The woman and the cats were gone. I hit the gas and did a U-turn. Nothing. No woman, no cats, only an open field of graves with nowhere to hide. The woman and the cats had vanished into thin air.

Becca and I checked out the Jewish section later that night, but other than hearing a few strange noises that could have been almost anything, we didn't experience anything unusual.

I'm going to stop short of telling you that we had seen the ghosts of a woman and her two cats that night in Patton Cemetery. *Just short.* Rare indeed are the times that a paranormal explanation is the *rational* explanation, but in the case of the woman and her two cats, it's the only thing that makes sense. The odds of our arriving at the Garden of Memories at the exact moment when a woman with two cats is standing in the exact spot where we had recorded an EVP asking about a cat are astronomical. The woman and her cats vanished in the middle of an open field of graves. She had nowhere to hide.

I can't tell you with any certainty that what we encountered that night was flesh or phantom. I can't tell you whether the woman was quick or dead. All that I *can* tell you is that if you go in search of the unknown, don't be surprised if you find it.

Chapter 3

Brush Lake Road: Munchkinland

Investigation: Franklin Cemetery and the
Legend of Munchkinland
Start date: August 12, 2006
Place: Franklin Cemetery in Eau Claire, Michigan

The Legend[4]

An old, dilapidated chapel sits at the T of Franklin Street and
Brush Lake Road in Eau Claire, Michigan. It is surrounded
by a small cemetery in which an unusually large number of
children and infants are interred. According to local legend,
the chapel and cemetery are haunted by the ghost of a young
boy who was murdered there by a former pastor. One of the
headstones in the cemetery glows with an eerie green light
after nightfall, and shadowy figures are seen moving through
the cemetery. The giggling ghosts of dead children can be
heard echoing throughout the cemetery late at night, and
other strange sounds and shadows are said to be abundant
and frequent. Other than this, little else is known about the

---

4. The Munchkinland page at StrangeUSA.com (www.strangeusa.com/
ViewLocation.aspx?locationid=5228) was a source for the background
information in this chapter.

spirits that haunt the cemetery or how the legend of Munchkinland came into being.

The Preliminary Investigation

WISP had planned to investigate Munchkinland for quite some time, but Sam and Amber were unavailable because they were still making preparations to sell their home in Illinois. Becca and I became restless and tired of waiting for our partners to return, so we decided to check out the cemetery on our own.

At the time, we had no way of knowing that decision would come back to haunt us in more ways than one.

As chief navigator, Becca plotted our course, as I read out loud to her the paranormal accounts of Munchkinland that I found online. Although the accounts varied in some ways, everyone who had ventured into Munchkinland after dark agreed on one thing: *the cemetery was the creepiest place they'd ever been.*

Becca and I were so intrigued by the accounts of paranormal activity at the cemetery that we made a huge mistake: we decided to forego scoping out the cemetery during the day as we had always done in the past. We were going to Munchkinland that very night! We found out too late that we weren't prepared for what we encountered at Munchkinland. Half of team WISP was about to step foot into the creepiest, most haunted place we had ever investigated.

Darkness Falls on Munchkinland

As we drove toward our destination, I was silently musing on what we might encounter at Munchkinland. Of all types of paranormal activity, the most disturbing to me are hauntings that involve the ghosts of dead children. The mere thought of ghost children sends a chill running up my spine, and the reports of childlike giggling frequently being heard in the cemetery after dark had already set the scene for a scary investigation.

Following Becca's directions, I maneuvered the van onto Brush Lake Road. Although the road was paved at first, it quickly dwindled into little more than a one-lane dirt trail that twisted and turned at random. There seemed to be no logic in the way Brush Lake Road had been laid out. We soon passed an old, dilapidated house surrounded by the rusting corpses of broken-down farm machinery. From their final resting places in the waist-high grass along the road, the machines seemed to be watching us drive by with their unblinking headlight eyes.

The area was growing more remote by the second, and I was growing more wary. Munchkinland was obviously nestled deep in the boondocks, far away from civilization (and help) if anything went wrong. When I pulled out my cell phone to check for a signal, its illuminated display informed me that I was most likely shit out of luck.

I was starting to get concerned for our safety. It wasn't ghosts that had me concerned, though; it was the local live people. *Who might be out here screwing around?* I asked myself. *Will we be able to handle any trouble as only half a team?*

I looked over at my wife, who was fiddling with the buttons on her video camera. I wasn't feeling very confident, and I was about to turn the van around and head for home when Munchkinland came into view. Becca was getting excited. It was too late to turn back. If anything dangerous awaited us in Franklin Cemetery, living or otherwise, we would have to face it alone.

As I pulled the van up to the far end of the cemetery and brought it to a stop, I saw something very interesting looming in the headlights: just as the local legends reported, a headstone near the back of the cemetery was giving off an eerie green glow. Suspicious that this phenomenon was natural, not supernatural, I switched off the van's headlights, and—*presto-chango*, the headstone went dark. Another car that drove by the cemetery later created the very same phenomenon. We determined that the type of stone the headstone was carved from was responsible for the phenomenon, not a paranormal presence. The case of paranormal activity creating the headstone's eerie green glow had been put to rest.

We had yet to even enter the cemetery, and the investigator in me was already growing skeptical of the legend of Munchkinland. The Witch in me, on the other hand, was clanging away on a warning bell inside my head. Even from the relative safety of the van, I sensed that there was something very wrong with Franklin Cemetery. Wrong in a way that makes a person's heart beat faster and his skin prickle with a cold chill. I glanced over at Becca. By the look on her face, it was obvious that she was sensing something wrong, too.

The darkness I had felt at Belle Gunness's former farm during an earlier investigation didn't hold a proverbial candle to the eerie sensations that were emanating from Munchkinland. The cemetery was foreboding and challenging at the same time, as if Munchkinland itself was daring us to step foot through its bent and rusted front gate. The feeling of a powerful unseen presence lurking inside the cemetery was overwhelming. So overwhelming, in fact, that Becca and I briefly discussed abandoning the investigation until we could return as a full team. But then our sense of adventure won out over caution. We gathered our gear and exited the van.

King of the Munchkins

As we approached the chapel and the gate that leads into the cemetery, I saw something that instantly raised my hackles: one side of the chapel's double-hung front doors had been kicked in and was hanging wide open. *Could somebody be inside?* I wondered. *A vagrant? Troublemakers? Were we going to get into trouble? Get hurt?* I told myself to be on guard at all times. I also noticed that there was graffiti spray-painted on the door that was still intact. I climbed the steps for a better look. What I saw in bright red lettering was the sentence, *I am the King of the Munchkins*. I read it to Becca, adding, "Teenage thrill-seekers." She agreed. Munchkinland was obviously a popular hangout for local miscreants who fancied themselves graffiti artists.

Stepping back from the doors, I scanned the chapel. It was in such disrepair that I was amazed it was still standing. I snapped a couple photos of the chapel with my digital camera, and—for just a moment—I saw someone or something standing inside the bell tower. I quickly scanned the photos I had just taken on the camera's LCD screen. Nothing unusual. Whoever or whatever was standing inside the bell tower had disappeared as suddenly as it had appeared. I asked Becca to fire up her video camera. If anything else appeared, I wanted to catch it on film.

Our equipment was at the ready. It was time to enter the cemetery and flush out the ghosts of Munchkinland.

But something at the gate made us hesitate. We were hearing strange sounds. They seemed to be coming from every direction. To our left, we were hearing a buzzing sound that was similar to the noise an electric generator makes. Behind us was a low, sweeping growl that flowed and churned as if caught up in a swift moving wind. Looking all around us, we stepped through the gate. The growling seemed to follow us. It was getting louder. Suddenly, something seemed to step between two large headstones and vanish. Becca took two steps backward. I reached for my flashlight. As I did, an unseen presence whispered the word *Vican* in my ear, and a loud grunt sounded somewhere close to us.

I told Becca to go for the gate, but she was already on her way. Strange noises were sounding all around us now. There was subtle, shadowy movement everywhere in the cemetery. I clicked on my flashlight and scanned the graveyard. Nothing but headstones.

Franklin Cemetery is small, no more than an acre in size, and most of the headstones are tiny. I was reasonably certain that whatever was on the prowl wasn't human. There simply weren't enough places to hide. Even though I was convinced this activity was paranormal, I wasn't about to take any more chances with my wife's safety. She was about ten feet away, back near the gate. "Head for the van," I said in my steadiest, most professional voice, and started walking toward her. From somewhere between us, a shrill *Woooo* sounded. The sound was so "classic ghost" in nature that if the area between us hadn't been empty, I would have been convinced that someone was playing a prank on us.

But no one was. There was no mistaking where the sound came from. Whatever had made the sound was very close to us, and yet nothing was there. At least, nothing we could see with our eyes. The ghosts of Franklin Cemetery obviously wanted to play, but I wasn't game. I joined Becca at the gate and escorted her to the van.

Then I decided to venture back inside the cemetery alone. I wouldn't remain there for long. As I stepped through the gate, the growling started up again. It was louder; it sounded angrier. It was unlike any earthly sound I had ever heard. It was all around me, and I knew for sure it could not be human in origin. The growling was circling me now, like a predator stalking its prey. When something peeked at me from behind a nearby headstone, I clicked on my flashlight and ran toward it. Nothing there. I heard two loud grunts. They were very close. There was another unearthly growl, and some unseen force brushed up hard against my legs.

I'd had enough. Whatever was stalking me felt dark and ferocious. Suddenly feeling alone and unguarded, I made for the gate and returned to the van.

The Uninvited

Becca and I decided that any further investigation of Munchkinland would be best performed as a full team. Our sense of adventure had just gotten the best of us. We realized that the paranormal activity inside the cemetery had begun so quickly that we hadn't had time to prepare ourselves metaphysically for the investigation. This, we assured ourselves, was a mistake that we would never make again, nor would we perform an investigation without first checking out the location during daylight hours.

As we drove away from Franklin Cemetery and the ghosts of Munchkinland, something quite extraordinary appeared in the van's headlights: a silver fox was trotting up the road about twenty yards ahead of us. Encounters with silver foxes are extremely rare, and even though the fox immediately skedaddled from view, we were delighted to see such a beautiful and interesting creature. But we wouldn't remain so enthusiastic for long.

As we neared the spot where Brush Lake Road changes back from dirt to pavement, Becca and I were simultaneously overcome with a powerful feeling of dread. Every hair on our bodies was standing at attention. We looked at each other. *What the fuck's going on?*

I checked in the rearview mirror, and what I saw almost made me drive off the road: someone or some*thing* was sitting in the back seat. I slammed on the brakes and switched on the van's overhead lights. There was nothing there. But even though whatever had been there—and we were sure it had been there—had vanished from sight, there was no mistaking the feeling that a powerful unseen presence still lingered. There was a darkness to the entity unlike anything I had ever felt before. Whatever had followed us out of Munchkinland was strong. *Very strong.*

In that moment I knew that persuading the entity to leave the van would be no easy task. It seemed quite comfortable right where it was. We would have to convince it otherwise. Our metaphysical skills were about to be put to the test.

Without hesitation, I reached for the one metaphysical tool I am never without during an investigation: my ritual knife. I held the knife before me and commanded the entity to leave the van. It resisted. I could actually see the shadows near the rear of the van shifting, as though something was thrashing around in the darkness. When I pushed again with all my willpower, the invisible entity pushed back. I was locked in a game of tug-o'-war with an angry ghost. I could feel Becca pushing at the entity, too. "Be ready to seal off the van once we get it out," I told her. If we were able to expel it, I sure didn't want it getting back inside.

Becca and I pushed and pushed. Finally, we began to feel the entity begin to weaken. Then, all at once, there was a loud, whooshing sound and we saw the shadows fly through the walls of the van. The unearthly presence was gone. Becca yelled, "Now!" and using every ounce of our remaining willpower, we focused the energy around us and placed a shield around the van. What had we experienced? I turned off the interior light, put the van in gear, and we drove home in silence.

Codename K9: Heidi, the Paranormal Detective

The very next morning after our nighttime investigation of Munchkinland, Becca and I decided to return to the cemetery during daylight hours to get a clearer picture of the burial grounds and a better feel for what we might be dealing with. We also decided to enlist the help of one of our closest friends: our family dog, Heidi. We had read some very interesting accounts of canines being used for paranormal investigations and were anxious to give it a try with our own pooch. The main theory behind using dogs to assist in investigating paranormal activity is that they are believed to possess a more heightened sense of otherworldly activity than we humans do. Could our faithful friend Heidi help us sniff out the ghosts of Munchkinland? We were about to find out.

After prepping our photographic equipment and audio recorders, we loaded Heidi into the van and made the long drive back to Eau Claire, Michigan, and Munchkinland. When we arrived, Becca and I immediately noticed that Munchkinland felt much more inviting during the daytime. But Heidi didn't share our feelings. Her normally happy and relaxed demeanor was replaced by obvious trepidation. She was nervous and skittish. Her natural curiosity was overcome by uncertainty, and she was extremely hesitant to leave the safety of the van, which wasn't like her at all. She is normally more than happy to go out for a jaunt and get some exercise. Not this time. Not in Munchkinland.

At my prodding, she finally jumped out of the van, but her paws had no sooner hit the ground than she started whining and pacing nervously back and forth. The whining was high-pitched and unlike any sound I had ever heard her make before. After I led her through Munchkinland's bent and rusted front gate and into the headstones, she finally started to relax, if only a little. But while the dog relaxed, Becca and I were growing more uncomfortable by the minute. Looking around us, we suddenly understood how Munchkinland had gotten its name and haunted reputation. We were surrounded by the graves of infants and young children.

The number of children's graves at Munchkinland is mind-boggling. Everywhere we turned, there was another and another and another. We had never encountered anything quite like it before. Intrigued and mystified by the large number of children's graves, Becca got out pen and paper and started wandering around among the tombstones to get an approximate count. At the same time, I turned on my digital recorder, and Heidi and I wandered off to try to record the voices of the dead.

As we approached the dilapidated chapel, I started hearing the high-pitched buzzing sound I'd heard the night before. When something whizzed by my head, I instantly knew what was making the sound. Bees. Walking closer to the chapel, I saw that the chimney had started separating from the building, and in the crevice between the chapel and the chimney was one of the largest beehives I had ever seen. There were hundreds, perhaps thousands, of bees swarming around the gap. This wasn't good. Becca, my wife and fellow investigator, is extremely allergic to bee stings. I tugged on Heidi's leash and started walking toward Becca to warn her to stay away from the back of the chapel.

Suddenly, Heidi froze in place and brought her ears to attention. She hunkered down and started to growl. There was something close by. Something she didn't care for one little bit.

Heidi and I were standing in the middle of the cemetery. I looked around, but I was having a hard time figuring out what had her so upset. Other than the three of us, Munchkinland was vacant, and I couldn't see so much as a squirrel or a bird nearby. Was my trusted canine companion sensing something paranormal? There was one surefire way to find out: I had to capture the voices of the dead on audio.

Becca was still quite a ways off, and, with no other humans in the cemetery, I knew this was my chance to record clear, uncontaminated audio. Paying close attention to Heidi and commenting on her behavior into my recorder, I led her through the headstones in search of the ghosts of Munchkinland. When she once again stopped abruptly and brought her ears to attention, I asked the ghosts a single question: "What do you think of my dog?"

When I played the audio back a few minutes later, I discovered that I had received an answer. But it wasn't very complimentary to my furry friend. I had captured a single word that seemed to be a direct response to my question: *Ugly.* The ghosts of Munchkinland apparently didn't much care for Heidi's physical appearance.

When Heidi and I rejoined Becca, she reported the number of children's graves she had been able to count. The number was staggering. She had counted no less than one hundred and three graves of infants and children nineteen years of age or under. In a cemetery less than one acre in size, that seemed like an unusually high number, a very dense population. Munchkinland also boasts well over thirty unmarked fieldstones, any number of which could potentially be the grave of a child.

When Becca and I returned home later that day and I started sifting through the audio I had recorded, I discovered that I had captured no fewer than ten anomalous voices, most of which seemed to be directly responding to my questions. Although none of the other voices I captured was discernible or anywhere near as clear and obvious as the one that pronounced my dog ugly, daytime EVP are a rare occurrence (as are other types of daytime paranormal phenomena), which begs the question, *Why?* A pet theory of mine is that the atmospheric conditions at night, as opposed to conditions during the day, are more conductive to paranormal activity and allow for stronger contact in much the same way that these same atmospheric conditions allow radio waves to travel farther at night.

The sheer number of daytime EVP I was able to capture in a short amount of time was quite intriguing. I was further intrigued by the fact that just before most of these voices were captured, Heidi had gone on full alert and was obviously aware of a presence.

There is no question in my mind that Heidi was sensing entities beyond our world and perhaps even picking up their voices with her sensitive canine hearing. But even though these findings were interesting and warranted further trials, Heidi's paranormal detective skills would have to be shelved for the time being.

Sam and Amber had finally completed their move to northern Indiana. It was time for team WISP to hunt the ghosts of Munchkinland in force.

The Little Lost Souls of Munchkinland

It felt wonderful to have the full team back together again. As we were gathering our equipment and making preparations for the return to Munchkinland, our spirits were high. We were pumped and primed for some serious ghost hunting. Our energy levels were also quite high, and we planned to put that energy to good use during the next evening's investigation.

After hearing what Becca and I had experienced during our first investigation of Munchkinland, Amber was excited and Sam was skeptical. This wasn't unexpected. Sam's skepticism is a grounding force and makes him an invaluable member of the team. But whether he was a good devil's advocate or not, I couldn't help but wonder if Sam would remain skeptical about Munchkinland after experiencing it firsthand.

As we drove toward our destination, we found ourselves on the trailing edge of a line of thunderstorms. Munchkinland was bound to be soggy, and the best we could hope was that the storms would have passed by the time we arrived. Fortunately for us, they did. As I pulled the van into Munchkinland and brought it to a stop, the rain had diminished to a light drizzle. We decided to venture into the cemetery but leave our equipment bagged until the rain stopped entirely.

As we approached the gate that led into the cemetery, we were filled with an overwhelming feeling that was a mixture of caution and excitement. The moisture in the ground mixed with the warm night air, creating a blanket of mist that crept over the cemetery. If Munchkinland wasn't haunted, tonight it certainly looked like it should be.

The drizzle was still falling at a pretty good rate, so we huddled together under a large oak tree near the entrance and scanned the cemetery for any signs of movement. There was nothing. Unlike our previous investigation, Munchkinland seemed calm tonight and (if you will forgive the unintentional pun) lifeless. No strange sounds, no movement. Even the front door of the chapel had been repaired and barred, so the possibility of someone lurking inside was remote. But as Sam and I were unpacking the cameras and audio equipment, Becca and Amber saw someone or *something* walk between two large headstones about fifteen feet in front of us. These were the same two headstones that Becca and I had seen something walk between on the night we had ventured into Munchkinland ourselves, as only half a team.

Now, after searching the area around the headstones thoroughly, we still found nothing. Since the movement around the headstones was repetitious, Becca suggested that the phenomenon might be caused by residual paranormal activity. We agreed, and Sam mounted one of our video cameras to a tripod to shoot footage of the headstones. At the same time, I placed puzzle pieces (from a Scooby-Doo puzzle, no less) on the headstone of a child's grave nearby, then sprinkled them with talcum powder. These puzzle pieces are what paranormal investigators know as *trigger objects*. The theory behind trigger objects is that ghosts can be attracted by interesting or familiar objects and feel compelled to investigate and/or move them.

Trigger objects can vary widely from one investigation (or investigator) to another, and are typically chosen after conducting extensive research into the background of the haunting. In other words, trigger objects are chosen based on what we learn about the ghost or ghosts that are believed to haunt a particular location. If the ghost is believed to be that of a person who died in the early years of the twentieth century, then the trigger objects used during the investigation are typically from that time period. Two examples would be old money or old jewelry. If the ghost is believed to be that of a modern-day child, then modern trigger objects such as a particular toy the child played with when alive can be used to trigger a response.

Since we had no specific information as to the time period in which the ghost or ghosts that haunt Munchkinland originated, the puzzle pieces seemed as good an idea as any to entice the disembodied spirit of a dead child to come out and play. Theoretically, their ghostly hands could potentially leave prints in the talcum powder. Once the puzzle pieces were in place, I snapped a digital photograph of the grave to use for reference when we started sifting through the evidence later on. I would snap a second photograph of the grave when it came time to wrap things up for the evening. If the puzzle pieces or talcum powder were disturbed during the investigation, we would have photographic evidence.

Sam finally got the video camera in a position he was satisfied with. He had no sooner pressed the record button when something at the far end of the cemetery screamed. Then something directly behind us screamed. The screams were identical. They were shrill and bloodcurdling. Clicking our flashlights on, we whirled around, looking for what had made the sounds. We could see nothing. We stood in silence, waiting for whatever had screamed to scream again. We didn't have to wait for long. From the far end of the cemetery came another scream, and then one more.

"What the hell is that?" I asked.

"It doesn't sound human," Amber added.

As it turned out, Amber was right. The screams weren't human in origin. We quickly discovered that they were the screams of animals. Birds, to be exact.

Scanning the edges of the cemetery with our flashlights, we finally saw unidentified fowl flitting about in the tree lines. Even though they were numerous, we couldn't get a close enough look at them to identify them. I wondered what kind of bird could make such a horrible sound. I further wondered if the screaming birds weren't in part respon-

sible for Munchkinland's haunted reputation. Certainly anyone inexperienced with wildlife might think the screaming
was paranormal. They even had seasoned investigators like
ourselves stumped for a few moments. But the birds soon
ceased their horrific screaming, and now it was time to move
on to more important matters than identifying the local wildlife. It was time to find the actual ghosts of Munchkinland.

Seeing in the Dark

Our WISP team decided it was time to try a new metaphysical technique for ghost hunting that we'd been developing
but had yet to field test. This new technique involved standing in a magic circle, raising a huge amount of energy as a
group, and then directing our cone of power into the ground
as a means to "light up" the entire area with energy, which
we hoped would allow us to pinpoint entities and/or pockets
of paranormal activity.

To start, we stood in a circle in the center of the cemetery and held hands. We closed our eyes and breathed deeply
of the night air. We opened our minds and our senses. We
focused on the goal. Soon we could feel the energy swirling
all around us. We pulled the energy in, feeling it flood our
bodies and our circle. Into this energy we mixed our willpower and our own energy, imprinting it with our goal: to
make contact and thin the veils between the worlds of the
living and the dead. We built the energy within ourselves,
strengthening it before passing it along to the next person
in the circle. The energy passed through us and around us,
encircling us, growing faster and stronger as it went. Soon
it was little more than a speeding blur of power and energy.

Then we raised the energy up, focusing it into a single powerful ball within the circle. I quickly knelt down and placed my hand on a fieldstone at my feet. My teammates and I focused and focused, building and raising the ball of energy, higher and higher. The energy reached its peak. It was time to release it.

As we had practiced it, we released that ball of energy and sent it plunging down into the ground. I felt it hit me like a white-hot wave of invisible light. I immediately sent it into the fieldstone beneath my hands, then sent it flowing into the cemetery. With my third eye, I saw the wave of energy wash over Munchkinland. This heightened visual phenomenon was unlike anything I had ever seen before. The energy wave pulsed and strobed, filling the cemetery with flashes of colored light. Flares of orange, red, and blue flowed forth, like vibrant and electric colors flowing into an old black-and-white photograph. What I was seeing was beautiful beyond description.

But I also saw something else. Something chilling. Within the colored flashes, I saw no fewer than five entities standing there. One of them was directly behind me. Without thinking, I stood up and grabbed the camera strapped around my neck. "There you are!" I raised the camera to snap a photo.

I never got it. Directly in front of me a loud *Uh!* sounded. My skin ran wild with gooseflesh. I felt something that can only be described as hot breath blowing over my face. Amber and Becca gasped. They had heard the sound, too. And Sam had heard it, though for the moment that didn't seem to matter. He was running toward the back of the cemetery like a man possessed. The three of us ran after him.

Shadows in the Night

The only normal illumination at Munchkinland is provided by a single streetlamp planted in the ground near the front of the chapel. As we came closer to Sam, we saw that he was standing near the back edge of the cemetery between the streetlamp and the tree line that surrounds all but the front of Munchkinland. He was staring at the tree line. As we came closer, our teammate took three quick steps backward. Something obviously had him jumpy.

"What's going on?" I called out.

"The shadows," he called back. "Look at the shadows."

We looked. They were moving. Large, humanoid shadows were walking. They were much too large to be the silhouettes of the screaming birds we had seen several minutes earlier. As Becca, Amber, and I watched from about twenty-five feet away, Sam clicked on his flashlight and scanned the rear of the cemetery. Nothing was there. He clicked it off, waited a few moments, and then repeated the process.

"I can't explain it," he called out to us. "There's movement all over the place back here, but when I turn on the light, whatever's making it vanishes."

We were about to walk closer to our teammate when, out of nowhere, an enormous shadow swept across the ground in front of him and enveloped the tree line. The shadow was taller than the trees. Near its top was a thin, muted aura of blue light. We looked at the area between Sam and the streetlight. Empty. There was nothing natural there that might account for this enormous shadow.

Then the shadow that had enveloped Sam and the tree line vanished as quickly as it had come.

Of all the strange things I've witnessed in my lifetime, this shadow comes close to topping the list. Its sheer size and the speed at which it had appeared were mind-blowing in their implications. This was easily one of the most impressive, one of the most convincing, displays of paranormal activity any of us had ever seen.

But the shadow had departed the cemetery, leaving behind no trace of its presence. There was nothing we could do now but ponder what it might have been. It was at that point Amber suggested that she should set up a video camera focused on the tree line and try to capture any further paranormal activity. Even though we agreed that was an excellent idea, she never got the chance. Suddenly, somewhere between Sam and the three of us, something unseen grunted. Somewhere in the darkness behind us a child started giggling.

Munchkinland had come to life.

Night of the Munchkins

The childlike giggling came from the farthest edge of the cemetery, approximately one hundred and fifty feet away from where we were standing. We immediately clicked off our flashlights and split into two groups, so that we could flank whatever it was from opposite directions. We slowly made our way through the darkness toward the sound, being careful not to trip over any of the fieldstones or smaller grave markers as we went. Our intention was to approach it in total darkness so that if a human prankster was doing the giggling, we could catch him or her in the act.

Becca and Sam were making their way toward the sound by way of the back edge of the cemetery, and Amber and

I were approaching from the front. As Amber and I neared the wrought-iron gate, a loud grunt sounded in the darkness directly in front of us. It sounded exactly like the grunting of a pig. We hesitated and strained to listen. Soon we could hear something outside the front gate. It was the low, sweeping growl I had heard the night Becca and I had ventured into Munchkinland on our own. It was slowly getting louder. Another grunt. Now it was behind us. We whirled, brandishing our flashlights like weapons. Nothing. Neither life nor movement behind us. Whatever had grunted at us was not of our world. Of that much we were certain.

We stood in silence for a few moments, waiting for the grunt to repeat. It didn't. All that remained was the unexplainable growl circling around Munchkinland's front gate like a predator, but even it was diminishing. We clicked off our flashlights and refocused on our original target: the giggling ghost children.

As Amber and I approached the far end of Munchkinland, we could just make out Sam's and Becca's silhouettes in the dim light. They were hunkered down near the leading edge of a short row of headstones. As we neared them, Sam held up his hand and motioned for us to stop where we were. We stopped and hunkered down as well, then waited in silence, listening to the sounds of the night.

Mixed in with the chirping of crickets and the light rustling of wind through the trees were soft, childlike voices. We could also see subtle movements in the shadows in front of us. Then we heard the sound of a young girl's laughter, followed by more laughter, slightly lower in pitch. The sounds were muted but recognizable. They were the sounds two children might make if they were enjoying a private joke and whispering and giggling quietly together.

I glanced at the digital audio recorder strapped to my arm to make sure that it was still recording. It was. It was time now to find out once and for all if the voices we were hearing were the voices of human children or ghosts. I slowly stood up and motioned to my teammates to encircle the area where the voices were originating. Moving as quickly as we could without making undue noise, we fanned out in a circle and stepped forward. The childlike voices continued. We were very close now. Flashlights at the ready, we swarmed in on our quarry. The darkness of Munchkinland flooded with light. The four of us stood in a tight circle, staring across at each other in disbelief. We were alone.

The ghosts of Munchkinland had outsmarted us again.

Altars for the Dead

Unable to think of any earthly explanation for the voices, we returned to the back edge of the cemetery where the enormous shadow had enveloped the tree line. We discovered something quite interesting: at the farthest corner of Munchkinland was a headstone in the shape of a bench. Arranged on the headstone in what appeared to be deliberate fashion were thirteen red tealight candles. The wicks of the candles had been burnt down to near nothingness. Around the candles, familiar symbols had been drawn in red and white chalk. This headstone had recently been used as an altar for an occult ritual.

It quickly became obvious to us that whoever had used this makeshift altar didn't have the vaguest clue what they were doing. The chalk symbols didn't make any sense at all. They seemed random and amateurish. Next to an Egyptian ankh, the head of Baphomet had been drawn. Next to a yin-yang symbol, an inverted pentagram. We easily deduced that whoever had set up the altar had watched *Rosemary's Baby* one too many times or maybe had picked up a copy of Anton LaVey's *Satanic Bible* at their local Barnes & Noble and had been attempting to impress their friends with a fly-by-night ritual.

But even so, we found the idea of Munchkinland being used as the site for a ritual quite intriguing. That Munchkinland is frequented by teenagers is well documented, and we began to wonder how many times the local striplings had ventured here with a crystal ball or Ouija board in hand in hopes of putting on a good show by attempting to make contact with the dead. We even grinned at the thought of an unprepared group of teens inadvertently conjuring up something they weren't prepared for. I recalled the warm summer nights of my youth and the many ghost stories my friends and I had shared with each other around a campfire at outside sleepovers, and I marveled at the thought of telling ghost stories at a creepy site like Munchkinland. I even got a chill or two just thinking about it.

We knew from our research that the back edge of the cemetery, where the ritual had taken place, was said to be one of the most paranormally active areas there. The enormous shadow that had engulfed the area earlier in the evening and the unprecedented amount of unexplainable movement along the tree line seemed to reinforce that belief. We spent the next hour investigating the back edge of the cemetery, but other than a few strange sounds that we couldn't pin down, nothing else unusual or paranormal took place. Running low on time and batteries, we finally fanned out through the haunted and hallowed ground in further search of the restless dead.

Darkness, Darkness

The remainder of our second night in Munchkinland was filled with paranormal activity. All around us we heard unidentifiable sounds and voices. Out of the corners of our eyes, we saw movement. Although their voices were vague and indiscernible, the dead were audibly responding to our questions. At one point something whispered the word *Vican* in Amber's ear, and she was catching brief glimpses of a presence that was following her around. *Vican* was the same word an unseen presence had spoken to me on the night Becca and I had investigated Munchkinland on our own. Amber didn't know this, and I was fascinated that we had both experienced the same voice on two separate occasions.

The activity continued until around two o'clock in the morning, at which time it stopped abruptly. The cemetery no longer felt like a living, breathing entity. Had the energy we'd infused into the ground finally run down? Or had the dead simply grown weary of playing with us? Either way, it was time for WISP to leave Munchkinland to those who called it home.

After gathering up most of our gear, we returned to the grave where I had placed the puzzle pieces earlier in the evening. I wanted to snap a second photograph and clean up the area. But when we reached the grave, we were fascinated and shocked by what we saw. The talcum powder had been disturbed. The puzzle pieces had been moved.

The Evidence

Video evidence: WISP was able to capture three pieces of video footage during our investigation of Munchkinland. The video evidence is as follows:

1. A high-definition video camera trained on the bell tower of the chapel recorded the manifestation of a black mass that momentarily took on humanoid form before fading away into nothingness. All doors leading in and out of the chapel had been locked during the entire evening. All windows had been permanently sealed. No earthy explanation can account for this apparition.

2. An infrared (IR) video camera trained on the two headstones where WISP had documented potentially repetitive paranormal activity captured a vaporous humanlike form stepping out from behind one of the headstones before moving toward, and disappearing behind, the second headstone. This activity happened very quickly, and therefore WISP cannot claim that the video footage is definitive proof of a paranormal presence. An earthly phenomenon may account for this interesting and unusual footage.

3. The same IR camera trained on the two headstones captured a portion of the enormous, wavelike shadow that engulfed the tree line at the rear edge of Munchkinland. Unfortunately, the angle of the video camera didn't allow for a panoramic view of the area and recorded neither the shadow's point of origin nor the tree line on which it came to rest. However, the muted

blue aura we saw on the top edge of the shadow is visible in the footage.

Photographic evidence: Although several of the still photographs taken during the investigation show interesting
anomalies, no definitive evidence of paranormal activity
was captured on camera.

Physical evidence: WISP was able to capture a single piece
of rare physical evidence during our investigation. After
examining the photographs of the puzzle pieces we had
placed on the child's grave, we discovered that the puzzle
pieces had in fact been moved. The talcum powder sprinkled on and around the puzzle pieces had been disturbed.
A partial handprint is apparent in the talcum powder.
Judging by the size of the handprint, it had been made by
the hand of a child.

Special note from the author: To avoid confusion, in the following examination of the audio evidence collected during the investigation of Munchkinland, the term *EVP* will
be used to describe the inaudible sounds and voices that
were captured on audio recorder as well as the sounds and
voices captured on audio recorder that were audible during the investigation.

Audio evidence: An overwhelming amount of audio evidence
was captured and documented during our investigation of
Munchkinland. The evidence is so overwhelming, in fact,
that listing every instance in chronological order here would
become lengthy, and a real chore to read and understand.
So for the sake of this report, let us forego the blow-by-blow
listing of EVP and instead discuss some of the more interesting audio phenomena WISP was able to capture.

Of all the EVP recorded at Munchkinland, only a handful of them contained discernible words. The discernible EVP were the words *ugly* (in reference to my dog, Heidi) recorded during the daytime investigation and the word *Vican* recorded during the two subsequent nighttime investigations. Sifting through numerous books and searching the Internet, I was unable to find any relevant reference to the word *Vican* (or any alternative spelling) whatsoever. Although numerous other voices were captured on audio during our investigations, the remainder of these EVP were too quiet to be determinant as paranormal activity and therefore had to be discarded as evidence.

All of the remaining EVP captured were screams, giggles, grunts, groans, growls, whispers, and so forth. Unlike most EVP that are only discovered during examination of the evidence, many of these EVP were audible at the time they were recorded. We found the audible EVP to be bone-chilling and fantastical in implication. Never before had the members of WISP encountered such an extraordinarily large number of audible EVP.

The childlike whispering and giggling was fascinating (not to mention downright creepy), but perhaps the most unnerving EVP occurred after we had raised the ball of energy and I was able to pinpoint the exact location of an otherworldly entity and elicit an audible response. This audible EVP was the loud grunt, the *Uh!* that sounded directly in my face after I pointed my camera at where I knew the entity was. I felt the energy force emitted by the entity's vocalization blow across my face. I clearly recall every hair on my body standing at attention.

The second audible EVP I recall with great clarity is the ghostly *Whoooo* that sounded directly in my ear on the night Becca and I ventured into Munchkinland on our own. The sound was so "classic Hollywood ghost" that if this audible EVP hadn't sounded so close to my ear, I would have had a hard time believing it wasn't another person pulling a prank.

The EVP recorded during our investigations of Munchkinland break every rule in the paranormal book. No earthly explanation can account for the abundant voices and strange sounds we captured on our audio recorders.

Conclusion

The four members of WISP concur that, inch for inch, Munchkinland is one of the most haunted locations in the Midwest, and perhaps one of the most haunted locations in the United States. At just over one acre in size, Munchkinland boasts the largest amount of paranormal activity that WISP has encountered and documented to date.

However, the paranormal activity there is also incredibly inconsistent. Over the last three years, WISP has investigated Munchkinland a total of nine times. But of those nine times, less than half of our investigations produced any evidence of paranormal activity. It would seem that there is some kind of paranormal "switch" governing the haunting of the cemetery. When there *is* paranormal activity occurring at Munchkinland, it is abundant and intense. When activity isn't occurring, Munchkinland is peaceful and quiet, almost serene. When Munchkinland is quiet, there is a calmness about it that seems to permeate a person and enter into their very soul. It is as if the graveyard itself were silently luring unsuspecting visitors forward, but our advice would be not to trust it.

WISP knows all too well that, quiet or active, Munchkinland is a paranormal trap patiently waiting to snap shut on anyone who dares to trespass on the ghosts who call it home.

Chapter 4

The Legend of Primrose Road

Investigation: Primrose Road and Adams Street Cemetery
Start date: October 13, 2007
Place: South Bend, Indiana

The Legend[5]

Of all the haunted legends in northern Indiana, the legend of Primrose Road in South Bend is by far the most beloved and well known to local residents. It is, in fact, difficult to find locals who haven't heard of this fascinating legend or even gone there to check it out for themselves. I grew up less than thirty miles away from Primrose Road and recall hearing about its legend from the time I was a young man. The legend has grown considerably over the years and centers on a series of supposedly supernatural events that many drivers and their passengers have claimed they've experienced while traveling down Primrose, particularly during nighttime hours.

---

5. Research sources: "Primrose Road" (www.angelfire.com/theforce/ haunted/primroseroad.htm) and the Indiana Ghost Trackers' website (www.indianaghosts.org).

These events include a phantom farmhouse that appears at random (but disappears before anyone can get close enough to investigate it), unearthly sounds (including the clomping of a spectral horse), and apparitions moving through the woods along the side of the road. Legend would also have us believe that a young woman was sacrificed near Primrose Road during an occult ritual, and that on the anniversary of her death, her ghost can be seen reenacting the ritual.

One of the most intriguing facets of the legend centers on vehicular trouble. Some locals insist that if you drive down Primrose Road at exactly twenty miles per hour, your car tires will be slashed, and that if you travel at exactly thirty miles per hour, your vehicle will simply die. In either case, you'll be forced to walk to get help, as cell phones are said to be useless on Primrose.

Adams Street Cemetery ties in with Primrose Road. It's only a few blocks away and is said to have ghostly happenings of its own. Although not nearly as intriguing as Primrose Road, Adams Street Cemetery is alleged to be haunted. Strange lights and unearthly mists have been reported to emanate from the cemetery after nightfall.

Even though much of the legend of Primrose Road seemed unlikely, the reports of occult rituals being performed in the area were enough to draw the interest of WISP. Investigating Primrose Road and Adams Street Cemetery for ourselves seemed like the perfectly natural thing to do.

The Daytime Investigations

Since Primrose Road is less than a thirty-minute drive from our base of operations, we decided to do some preliminary scouting in the area during daylight hours to assess the lay of the land. Our resident navigator, Becca, mapped out our course, and with digital camera in hand, we headed to South Bend, Indiana, and Primrose Road. We arrived at our destination without incident, but as I turned the van onto Primrose Road, I was immediately disturbed by what I was seeing. Instead of the creepy stretch of haunted roadway the legend promised, the area was a suburban hell.

My immediate reaction was that we were on the wrong road, but my teammates encouraged me to drive on. A mile or so down the road, the crowded neighborhoods began to thin, then disappeared altogether. It was at this point that Primrose changed from paved road to dirt and gravel, while overhead a canopy of trees created a tunnel that was creepy and ominous, even in broad daylight. It was at that point that Becca and Sam looked at their cell phones. No signal whatsoever. Was there some supernatural force at work suppressing the cell phone signals? Was the legend of Primrose Road coming true?

Considering Primrose's relatively remote location and the thick canopy of trees, supernatural forces seemed unlikely. More likely was that ordinary, earthly forces were to blame for the lack of any signal.

As we continued our slow drive along Primrose's rough gravel surface, I asked my teammates to open themselves to sensing any unusual feelings or sensations and report anything they felt to the rest of us. About half a mile down the road, Amber and I simultaneously experienced an uneasy feeling and felt a profound sense of sadness that seemed to be emanating from an area of the woods nearby. I had reset the van's trip meter at the point where Primrose changed from pavement to dirt and gravel, and I now made note of the mileage so that we could pinpoint this exact location on our return trip later in the evening. Sensing nothing else unusual, I decided to test another part of the legend of Primrose Road: vehicular trouble.

Even though it was still daylight, my curiosity got the better of me. I brought the van up to exactly twenty miles an hour and maintained that speed for approximately half a mile. Nothing happened. This didn't surprise me, as I really didn't suspect that anything would happen. That part of the legend seemed so far-fetched that the mere thought of it put a cynical grin on my face. I applied more pressure to the gas pedal and brought the van up to exactly thirty miles an hour. The surface of Primrose Road is anything but smooth, and even though the increase in speed made for quite a bumpy ride, I somehow managed to keep the van at an even thirty miles an hour. Soon we saw a stop sign in the distance with nothing but woods beyond it. We were quickly running out of supposedly haunted road.

I was just about to take my foot off the gas pedal and apply the brake when something happened that I had never before experienced with my van. It shimmied, coughed, and acted as though it were going to stop running altogether. Although the van's engine never completely died, I had to put the transmission into neutral and coax the gas pedal to keep the engine running. The van's forward momentum was enough to allow us to reach the stop sign, and, as we did, the van started to idle normally. We had a few moments of uncomfortable silence in the van. It was as if we were all waiting for something *really* bizarre to happen. Nothing did. Sam asked me if I had ever had trouble with the van dying before. My truthful answer was no. The van had never given me a lick of trouble before now, and the shimmy and cough were just plain weird. Having neither a natural or supernatural explanation for the van's strange behavior, I turned onto Adams Street and we went in search of the cemetery.

Adams Street Cemetery

Adams Street Cemetery, also known as Portage Prairie Cemetery, turned out to only be a short drive from Primrose Road. The written accounts by previous ghost hunters only described strange lights and ghostly mists, so we really didn't expect to see much of anything during daylight hours. Upon first sight, Adams Street Cemetery appeared to be very old. There were reportedly graves in the cemetery that dated back to the early nineteenth century, and, judging from the dilapidated condition of the cemetery's iron gate and a large number of the tombstones, this seemed likely. The cemetery is located on the outskirts of several mid-sized neighborhoods, which made me immediately suspect that the strange lights and ghostly mists were of earthly origin. There was no way to validate my suspicions until after nightfall, however, so I asked my teammates to disperse themselves throughout the graveyard and see if they could pick up on anything unusual.

After about fifteen minutes of looking around and inspecting tombstones, no one had anything to report. Adams

Street Cemetery seemed, in fact, oddly devoid of other-worldly feelings or sensations. Amber did pick up on a single tombstone that seemed to emanate a sensation of sadness very similar to the sensation we'd felt on Primrose Road, though it felt weak in comparison.

The oldest grave marker we could find with a legible inscription was dated 1856, and though some tombstones appeared to be even older, time and weathering had taken their toll on the stone surfaces. Without detailed burial records, reports of graves in Adams Street Cemetery dating back even earlier in the nineteenth century could be neither proved nor disproved. It was getting late in the afternoon at that point, so we decided to head back to our base of operations to prepare for our late-night incursions into Primrose Road and Adams Street Cemetery. Little did we know that one of these two locations would become an entirely different world after nightfall, a world crawling with ghosts and paranormal activity.

Darkness Falls on Primrose Road

Nighttime had come at long last. It was time to gather up our ghost-hunting gear, clear our minds, and return to Primrose Road. As the women loaded up the van, Sam and I spoke quietly about something odd that had happened to the two of us at a restaurant earlier in the day, something we were debating about whether or not to discuss with the women. We had both simultaneously experienced a premonition at the restaurant that had us deeply concerned—a premonition of a shotgun blast on Primrose Road. Were our premonitions significant enough for us to call off the investigation?

Even though premonitions of a shotgun blast were obviously nothing to shrug off, we sensed no inherent danger to the team. So we decided to proceed with the investigation as planned. Something about the premonitions felt residual, as if it were something that had already happened rather than was going to happen. Deciding it would be in the team's best interest not to worry the other two, we kept the premonitions to ourselves and headed for Primrose Road.

It was a typically chilly October night in northern Indiana, and as we approached Primrose Road, a dense mist greeted us. Fingerlike wisps of vapor poured out of the woods and disappeared into the dark cornfields along the roadside. The mist was nothing more than one of Mother Nature's parlor tricks, but it added greatly to the ominous look and feel of the Primrose area. I had a pretty clear picture in my mind of what Primrose Road would look like after nightfall, and as I turned the van onto the rough gravel surface, I wasn't disappointed. If Primrose Road *wasn't* haunted, I said to myself, it certainly looked as though it should be. The thick tunnel of trees towering overhead was creepy enough during the day, but after dark Primrose Road became an entirely different world. It was just plain eerie.

Shaking off my wonderment, I reset the van's trip meter and we proceeded up the road to where Amber and I had experienced the sense of great sadness earlier in the day. When we arrived, I pulled the van off to the side of the road, turned off the headlights, and killed the engine. I grabbed my flashlight and was about to exit the van when my wife, Becca, latched onto my arm. "Marcus, we have to get out of here *right now.*"

I turned on the flashlight and shone it into the back of the van. What I saw was deeply disturbing. Becca and Amber were both shaking. Their faces were pale, their eyes bleak. "*Something's wrong.* You have to get us out of here," Amber said.

I myself sensed nothing unusual, but rather than question my teammates, I started the van and continued the slow drive down Primrose Road. After a few moments of uncomfortable silence, I asked the girls what had happened. They both stated that for some inexplicable reason they had experienced an overpowering sensation of foreboding in the very spot where I had parked the van. They agreed that the sensation had vanished as soon as we were clear of that spot and now they were okay to continue with the investigation. Even though the girls seemed genuinely stable, I suggested that it was probably a good idea to get clear of Primrose for a while. "Let's check out Adams Street Cemetery," I suggested. They enthusiastically agreed.

Nighttime in Adams Street Cemetery

Adams Street Cemetery is nestled in the midst of several mid-sized neighborhoods, a fact that made me suspicious of the accounts of paranormal activity in the cemetery. As we entered the dimly lit graveyard, all four of us felt the same thing that we had felt earlier in the day: absolutely nothing. Even after nightfall, Adams Street Cemetery held no otherworldly feelings and sensations. Even though the cemetery seemed to offer little promise of authentic paranormal activity, I still asked the team to walk around to see if they could pick up on anything unusual.

After some thirty minutes, no one had anything to report. Becca had, however, snapped quite a few digital photos, and when we looked at some of them, we seemed to see the purported strange lights. Using the headstones as markers, we were able to pinpoint the exact locations where the photographs had been taken.

Unsurprisingly, the "strange lights" turned out to be nothing more sinister than houselights and streetlamps shining through the trees and bushes from the surrounding neighborhoods. "But what about the strange mists?" I asked.

As if in response to my question, a car sitting in a driveway across the street from the cemetery roared to life. A thick cloud of blue-gray exhaust rolled over the road and swirled about the edge of the graveyard. Reports of ghostly lights and strange mists in Adams Street Cemetery were laid to rest. With nothing at all unusual happening at the graveyard, team WISP decided that it was time to head back to Primrose Road and further our investigation there. What we encountered upon our return made the sensation of foreboding the girls had experienced earlier feel weak in comparison.

SPECIAL NOTE FROM THE AUTHOR

Before we go on, let's discuss what is known as "energy manipulation." In the following account, you will read about how at one point I used energy manipulation in an attempt to make contact with the dead. Unless you have a deep understanding of occult practices, Witchcraft in particular, the concept of energy manipulation may seem a bit preposterous, perhaps even laughable. I assure you that not only is energy manipulation real, but an adept practitioner can use it to affect immediate change.

Differing forms of occult energy manipulation include creating an area of protected or "safe" space, creating balls or "bubbles" of energy, and thinning the walls between the worlds of the living and the dead, the seen and the unseen. Even though manipulated energy typically cannot be seen with the naked eye, it can be felt and, in some cases, measured. In recent years there have been scientific attempts to quantify psychic energy that have produced some interesting results. If you wish to investigate some of the scientific approaches being used to measure psychic energy, I suggest Googling the keywords *scientific verification of psychic energy* (or something similar). Read some of the hits you get. You might be surprised.

When placed in its proper context, occult energy manipulation isn't difficult to understand. Science tells us that literally everything is made up of energy. You are energy; I am energy; your dining room table is energy; our computers are energy; the ground beneath our feet is energy. These energies simply manifest in different forms. The way an occult practitioner manipulates energy is not all that dissimilar from the way you yourself manipulate energy. Like the energy itself, we use different forms of manipulation.

Try this. Imagine yourself picking up a baseball (a seemingly solid ball of energy) and holding it in your hand. What are some of the things you could do with the baseball? You can carry it around in your pocket or use it to play catch with your child in the backyard. You can use it to smash out a window or throw it into a puddle of water to see how big a splash it would make. In very much the same way that you could use the baseball to affect a series of outcomes or create change in the physical world, occult practitioners use their minds and willpower to gather what is known as "universal energy" and use it as they see fit.

If you don't believe that such energy manipulation is possible, that's just fine by me. We all have our own beliefs and opinions, and I have no desire to change yours. I will, however, point out that belief is a very powerful thing. If you disbelieve in occult energy manipulation, your disbelief is precisely why you would fail if you were to attempt it—just as I would fail at anything I didn't believe that I could accomplish.

Paranormal investigators, be they Christian or Witch, scientist or psychic, amateur or professional, all believe in the same thing: *ghosts exist*. It is this belief, no matter what process is used for investigation, that keeps us in search of the unknown. It is this belief that keeps us searching for something that we know exists but can't quite put our fingers on, something more than what we can see with our eyes and touch with our hands. Like occult energy manipulation, ghosts are something most of us don't quite understand. They're supernatural.

The Ghosts of Primrose Road

As we left Adams Street Cemetery and made our way back to Primrose Road, I could feel how low our morale was. The cemetery investigation had been a complete wash, and thus far the only evidence of paranormal activity was the feeling of extreme foreboding that Becca and Amber had experienced on Primrose Road earlier in the evening. *Not a very promising start*, I thought. In an attempt to lighten the mood, Sam pulled out his cell phone and made a jovial remark about "ghosts making phone calls." Not to be outdone, Becca pulled out her phone, and the two of them began exchanging lighthearted quips about cell phone signals and the legend of Primrose Road. Soon enough, the entire team was laughing over the silliness of that part of the legend.

Well, at least we were laughing for a few moments. As I pulled the van back onto Primrose's rough gravel surface, the laughter came to an abrupt halt. In the eerie silence that replaced it, I stopped the van and turned on the interior lights. Becca and Sam were staring at their cell phones as though they'd never seen them before. "Holy shit!" Becca exclaimed. "Yours, too?" she asked Sam, thrusting her phone in his direction. "Yep. Mine, too," Sam quietly responded. The batteries on both of their cell phones had simultaneously drained from full charge down to nothing in a matter of seconds. Both phones were inoperable. It seemed that the spirits of Primrose Road didn't appreciate being laughed at.

In silence, I pulled the van over to the shoulder of the road and killed the engine. Even though no one was talking, it was obvious that the collective mindset of team WISP had taken on a more serious tone. With newfound eagerness and a determination to find *something*, we gathered our ghost-hunting gear and exited the van.

The absolute blackness of Primrose Road after nightfall is difficult to comprehend unless you have experienced this kind of darkness firsthand. Without a source of light, you really cannot see your own hand in front of your face. I wanted to keep the use of flashlights to a minimum, so I queried the rest of the team as to how they felt about using the four-way flashers on the van to provide us with a source of low-level illumination. My suggestion was met with a great deal of resistance. My teammates agreed that using the van's flashers would add a safety factor to the investigation, but Becca and Amber were concerned that the flashing lights would contaminate the video footage and still photographs they planned on taking. I submitted to their logic, clipped my digital recorder to my leather coat, and we began a slow walk down Primrose Road.

After several minutes of walking, I could see headlights coming toward us in the distance. I signaled the rest of the team to move onto the shoulder of the road and wait there until the approaching vehicle had passed. Becca had begun snapping digital photographs as soon as we had started walking. Several of the photos in the viewfinder revealed orbs, which were nothing more than airborne dust particles illuminated by the flash of the camera, but Becca was enjoying herself just the same.

As the vehicle approached, Becca readied her camera for another shot. Just as the vehicle passed us by, she snapped a photo, looked at the viewfinder, and started laughing her ass off. "You've got to see this," she giggled. "It's an amateur ghost hunter's wet dream!" We gathered around her, took a look, and began laughing. The camera's viewfinder revealed thousands, perhaps millions, of orbs. "Cool!" I exclaimed, shaking my head at the thought of anyone taking the picture seriously. At that moment, I noticed the headlights of a second vehicle moving down the road toward us. "Are we ever going to get any peace and quiet?" I asked aloud.

What happened next was priceless.

As the vehicle approached us, it began to slow down, and in my mind I started rehearsing my "explanation to the police" and "we don't need any help" monologues. Instead of a police car or a concerned motorist, however, an old, dark blue Chevy Blazer pulled up alongside us and came to a stop. Someone inside the Blazer rolled down the passenger-side window, and an eager young voice asked, "Are you out here ghost hunting, too?"

I clicked on my flashlight and shone it inside the Blazer. What I saw put a proverbial ear-to-ear grin on my face. Manning the wheel of the Blazer was a rather excited-looking adolescent male of approximately seventeen years of age. Sitting next to him in the passenger seat was his young girlfriend, who was doing her best not to look frightened. She was smiling, but her eyes told a different story. I informed the young man that we were indeed conducting a paranormal investigation and that we hadn't found anything yet. After asking team WISP a few questions about what we knew of Primrose Road, the youth politely excused himself, managed to get the Blazer turned around, and headed back down Primrose the way he had driven in.

About twenty-five feet down the road, he stopped the vehicle and opened the door. In the glow of the Blazer's headlights, he inched his way toward the edge of the woods. His hand never left the car door. Moments later, he turned his attention back to his vehicle and seemed to be responding to something his girlfriend was saying to him. One second later, he jumped back inside the Blazer, slammed the door, and sped away.

After a few remarks from the WISP women about "how cute it was" for the young man to take his girlfriend out for a little scare, we returned our attention to the task at hand and continued our slow walk down Primrose Road. Before long, I started getting an uneasy feeling that we were being watched. A loud snorting sound suddenly emanated from somewhere close to us in the woods. All four of us froze in our tracks.

"What the hell was that?" I whispered just before a second loud snort shot out from the opposite side of the road. Silent and unmoving, we stood in the middle of Primrose Road listening to the sounds of the night. Two more snorts came out of the darkness, sounding closer to us. As if we were reading each other's minds, all four of us clicked on our flashlights in unison and scanned the tree line for any signs of life. Nothing. At least nothing that was visible in the beams of our flashlights. "That sounded like a horse," I said. My teammates agreed. Even though there was probably a rational, earthly explanation for the snorting sounds, the scenario was disturbing. Other than the snorts, there were no other sounds of any kind around us. Not so much as the snapping of a twig or rustling of a leaf. Whatever was in the woods making those snorting sounds certainly didn't seem to be afraid of our flashlights. Or of us. If an animal was snorting, it never moved. Not once.

We finally deduced that whatever had been snorting was large, probably the size of a full-grown buck or a horse. The problem was that explanation didn't make any sense. I have come across many deer in the woods after nightfall, and I know that a deer running through the forest is anything but quiet. Deer can remain motionless for a long time, but as soon as they sense the presence of a group of humans talking and wielding a flashlight, it's *adios, muchachos*.

The horse theory didn't work, either. The odds of a horse standing completely still in the woods after nightfall, snorting and making no other sounds of any kind, were remote in the extreme. Nothing explained why the snorting seemed to emanate from both sides of the road, either. Whatever had snorted at us in the darkness seemed intent on remaining mysterious. With no rational explanation at hand, we continued our increasingly strange walk down Primrose Road.

As we walked, Becca kept snapping photographs and Amber tried to pick up on any strange feelings or sensations. Nothing seemed to be registering on any of our ghost-hunting gear, however, and it began to seem that other than the inexplicable draining of the cell phone batteries and the strange snorting sounds, nothing unusual was happening on Primrose Road. I was about to suggest to my teammates that we implement a metaphysical approach to making contact, when all at once my body seemed to become incredibly heavy and the air around me grew thick. I felt as though I were walking through an invisible wall of honey.

"There's something here," I said to my teammates. "The air just got heavy." At that very moment we came upon an opening in the woods that revealed a small, dimly lit field.

What happened next left little doubt in our minds that Primrose Road is one of the most haunted places in northern Indiana.

It's difficult for me to put what happened into words, but I'll do my best. As we moved toward the opening in the tree line, I started hearing what sounded like very faint whispering voices. I stopped and stood motionless, concentrating on the sounds, when all at once I felt the presence of a ghostly entity. It was attempting to manifest itself in the field. And it wasn't alone. I felt the presence of another entity, and then another. All told, I sensed between seven and nine distinct, tightly grouped entities approximately ten yards away from us in the field. The sheer number of entities was overwhelming. For a moment, I questioned my grip on reality. I focused my eyes, ears, and mind. "Are they really there?" I asked myself.

The answer was *yes*. Their quiet whispering voices were growing louder. I was catching glimpses of their shadowy figures moving around the dimly lit field. The easiest way to explain what the entities looked like is to say that they seemed to be slightly out of phase with the world of the living. They had definite outlines and forms, but they seemed to flux and change like shadows being projected onto a wall by flickering candlelight. I spoke in a loud, firm voice and said, "Show yourselves to me."

The whispering voices seemed to grow louder; the shadowy forms became more active. Was this in response to my request? I decided it was time to test a theory about spectral entities. It was time to put my metaphysical skills to the test.

It is widely stated—and believed—that ghosts need to draw upon an energy source other than their own to materialize on the earthly plane. In an attempt to prove this theory, I created a large ball of energy and concentrated it in the field directly in front of the shadowy figures. It seemed to have an effect, although not quite the one I was hoping for.

I stated aloud to the entities that I had created the ball of energy and that they were welcome to use it if they needed to. I kept my mind and will focused on the energy ball in case it needed reinforcing. Within minutes, I felt Amber's hand on my shoulder. She was also projecting energy into the ball, helping to keep it strong and stable. Even though none of the entities fully manifested, the visuals occurring within the energy ball were impressive to behold. It was obvious that the entities were interested in the energy ball, but it was also obvious that they didn't understand what to do with it.

The best way to describe what we were seeing is to compare the energy ball to a huge, water-filled snow globe that is slowly being injected with black ink. The shadows and forms in the ball of energy seemed to be fluid and flowing, whereas the shadows outside the ball seemed to be static and unchanging. As I repeated my request that the entities show themselves, the activity inside the energy ball increased significantly. I could sense that the ghostly entities were attempting to use the available energy. The activity inside the ball increased exponentially ... and then, just as I felt that one or more of the entities might actually manifest, they vanished without a trace. Their whispering voices and flowing forms disappeared into the darkness. The overwhelming sensation of a powerful supernatural presence disappeared as quickly as it had arrived.

I stood with my teammates on the shoulder of the road. We could hardly believe what we had just experienced. The question of whether or not Primrose Road was haunted had just been answered.

We still stood there, but after several minutes of quiet, reflective surveillance of the surrounding area, we saw nothing else. Whatever had visited us on that dark and lonely stretch of Primrose Road showed no indication of returning. We decided to head back to where the van was parked and investigate the opposite end of the roadway. As we walked, Becca continued snapping digital photographs and I kept calling out to the ghosts to come back out of hiding. Nothing was registering on our ghost-hunting gear, and there was no response to my vocal pleas for further contact.

After several minutes of walking, we passed the van and came to the last stretch of Primrose Road, which we had yet to investigate. We had only traveled a short distance past where the van was parked when things started getting weird again. Amber said she was catching glimpses of ghostly flashes of light moving through the woods. Becca complained of an intensifying feeling of unease. A minute later, she added that she felt strangely unwelcome in this section of Primrose Road and that each time she snapped a photograph, the feeling got stronger.

I asked Amber if the flashes of light she was seeing could possibly be aftereffects caused by the flash from Becca's camera. She replied that she was uncertain about what might be causing the strange flashes, but that she was also beginning to feel unwelcome here. A few moments later, the sensation of being unwelcome became so intense for them that Becca and Amber stated that they could no longer continue with the investigation. Becca asked me for the car keys, and she and Amber returned to the relative safety of the van.

Unlike the women, Sam and I felt completely at ease in that section of Primrose Road. Well, at least we felt at ease for a minute or two. After walking a few more blocks down the road in the darkness, I clicked on my flashlight and scanned the tree line and roadway before us. I told Sam I believed we were very close to where I had parked the van when we had first arrived earlier in the evening. He nodded and said that Amber and Becca might have picked up on the same feeling of foreboding that had forced us to evacuate Primrose Road.

Then I started hearing whispers again, so I turned off my flashlight and listened intently. The voices grew louder. Far ahead of us in the distance, Sam and I could see lights moving toward us through the woods. Aha! These voices and lights were of earthly origin. It was apparent that a small group of people with flashlights was approaching. I was about to suggest to Sam that the advancing group might be another team of ghost hunters and that we should check them out, when all at once an overpowering sensation of danger washed over me in an invisible wave. Sam also felt it.

At that very moment the realization hit home. Sam and I simultaneously whispered the same two words to each other in the darkness: *shotgun blast*. There was little doubt in our minds that the premonitions of a shotgun blast on Primrose Road we had both experienced earlier in the day had a strong chance of becoming a reality. We were almost certain that if we remained where we were, one or more of us were going to get hurt. Maybe worse. We felt a sudden sense of urgency. Our strong instinct of survival kicked in.

The woods that surround Primrose Road are private property, and we knew it. Bright orange *No Trespassing* signs were posted all along the shoulders of the road. Even though not a single member of our team had violated the sanctity of the property line, the sensation of impending danger was unrelenting.

Moving as quickly and quietly as we could, Sam and I made a dash for the van. In this case, discretion was indeed the better part of valor. Team WISP made a hasty escape from the humans and the spirits that haunt Primrose Road.

The Evidence

Photographic evidence: No photographic evidence of para-normal activity was captured during the investigation.

Audio evidence: Although indiscernible and barely audible at the time, multiple EVP were captured on our digital recorders during the investigation of Primrose Road. We were able to capture six distinct EVP at the scene. All six recorded instances sound as though they are emanating from different entities. What follows are WISP's interpretations of the EVP.

Primrose Road EVP in Chronological Order of Their Capture

1. Investigator: "We're not here to hurt you or anything." A woman's voice can be heard saying, "Won't hurt you." An English accent is detectable in this voice.

2. Investigator: "Show yourself to me." At this point, three separate EVP were captured on the recorder. The first voice, the voice of a young (male?) child, can be heard saying, "Can't now." The second voice, a male, can be heard saying, "Catch up." The third voice, also a male, can be heard saying, "Important." This voice is distinct from the others and has an almost electronic quality. Later, listening carefully to the audio file, we could hear the voice saying the word *important* a second time. Interestingly, the second time the voice sounds, the investigator pauses mid-word, as if interrupted by the disembodied voice.

3. Investigator: "Can you say that again, please?" Disembodied voice: "Never."

4. A disembodied voice says, "Dig bog," or "Big dog," right before the investigator says, "Very dark in here." This voice is much lower in timbre than the others and at first was difficult to hear. Of all the EVP captured during the investigation, however, this voice is perhaps the most disturbing, due to its dark, animal-like quality.

Conclusion

Primrose Road seems to live up to its haunted reputation. Although no photographic evidence was captured during the investigation, we feel the audio evidence speaks for itself (no pun intended) and backs up many of the experiences that we believe were paranormal in nature. Even so, many of the team's experiences, however odd, were explainable in natural terms and cannot be considered evidence of paranormal activity—although some of our experiences (the sudden draining of the cell phone batteries, the strange snorting sounds in the woods, and the vehicular trouble) seemed to reinforce the legend of Primrose Road.

By far, the most disturbing experience on Primrose Road was the encounter with the multiple spectral entities. Even though the entities didn't seem threatening, their number gave us pause and left us with many unanswered questions, not the least of which is, "Were all of the entities indigenous to Primrose Road?"

As practitioners of the occult arts, we know it is not uncommon for ghosts and spirits to be drawn to the enhanced aura of energy that naturally surrounds us. Even though a standard part of WISP's operational procedure for paranormal investigation involves putting a barrier in place to keep non-indigenous entities from entering and contaminating an investigation site, the encounter on Primrose Road left us questioning the effectiveness of the barrier in this particular instance. The members of WISP mutually agree that some, but not all, of the entities we encountered on Primrose Road were indigenous to the area.

Another fascinating and somewhat disturbing facet to the encounter is the verbal interaction that took place between the spectral entities and myself. Five of the six EVP captured at the scene reveal direct responses from the entities to our questions and requests. This interaction indicates that the haunting of Primrose Road is intelligent rather than residual, thus demonstrating an unusually high number of intelligent, self-aware entities concentrated in a single area.

Last is the area of Primrose Road that seemed to continually generate sensations of sadness and foreboding, and made two of us feel unwelcome. This area of Primrose is also where Sam and I felt endangered by the possibility of our premonitions of a shotgun blast becoming a reality. Whatever haunts that stretch of Primrose Road obviously doesn't want to be disturbed. In my opinion, whatever is prowling that stretch of roadway, be it human or specter, natural or supernatural, is better left alone.

Overall, our investigation of Primrose Road was a fascinating and productive glimpse into the world of the supernatural. There is no question in my mind that Primrose Road is haunted and is quite possibly a hotbed of paranormal activity.

For me personally, however, the truly wondrous encounter on Primrose Road wasn't with the dead, but with the living. Although I experienced many fascinating supernatural events during the investigation, I would be hard-pressed not to trade them all for the chance encounter with the teenage boy and his girlfriend in the Chevy Blazer. The world of ghosts and the supernatural is magical without question, but even more magical still are the memories of my own younger days, when I took my girlfriend out for a late-night drive down a haunted stretch of road in hopes that she would become frightened and snuggle close to me. That's the stuff legends are made of.

Chapter 5

North 25th Street:
Jeffrey Dahmer

Investigation: Former site of Jeffrey Dahmer's
apartment building

Start date: June 14, 2008

Place: Milwaukee, Wisconsin

The Macabre History of
Serial Killer Jeffrey Dahmer[6]

There probably isn't a man or woman in the Western Hemisphere who hasn't heard of Jeffrey Lionel Dahmer. Between 1978 and 1991, Dahmer murdered seventeen men and boys, most of whom were of African or Asian descent. Many of Dahmer's murders were exceedingly gruesome, involving torture, rape, necrophilia, dismemberment, and even cannibalism.

Dahmer's early childhood seemed normal, at least until he reached the age of ten. At this point, he started withdrawing from normal childhood activities and became more and more interested in dead things. He was known to ride his bicycle

---

6. Online sources that helped me in my research include "Jeffrey Dahmer Biography," *Biography.com* (www.biography.com/articles/Jeffrey-Dahmer -9264755); and Charles Montaldo, "Profile of Serial Killer Jeffrey Dahmer," *About.com* (http://crime.about.com/od/serial/a/dahmer.htm).

around the neighborhood in which he lived, collecting the bodies of dead animals, which he took back to his home to dissect. Many experts believe that it was at this point in his life that an insatiable taste for the gruesome and bizarre began to take hold inside him.

Dahmer committed his first murder in the summer of 1978, while he was still living with his father in Bath, Ohio. He picked up a young hitchhiker named Steven Hicks, and, after taking him back to his father's home and having sex with him, bludgeoned him to death with a barbell. Dahmer didn't kill again until nine years later, when his victim was Steven Tuomi. After the murder of Tuomi, Dahmer continued to kill sporadically, usually picking up his victims in gay bars and murdering them after having sex with them.

In May of 1990, Dahmer moved into Apartment 213 of 924 North 25th Street in Milwaukee, Wisconsin, where he killed the rest of his known victims. By the early summer of 1991, Dahmer was murdering approximately one person every week.

Dahmer was arrested on July 22, 1991, when Tracy Edwards, one of his intended victims, escaped from his apartment and waved down officers Robert Rauth and Rolf Mueller of the Milwaukee Police Department. After Edwards explained to the officers that Dahmer had tried to subdue him with handcuffs and threatened him with a butcher knife, Rauth and Mueller went to Dahmer's apartment to question him. At first Dahmer seemed normal and treated the officers kindly, but they quickly became suspicious and forced their way into his apartment. What they discovered inside was one of the most grisly crime scenes in American history.

Checking the bedroom where Tracy Edwards claimed Dahmer had threatened him with a knife, one of the officers discovered photographs of mutilated bodies. He called for his partner to arrest Dahmer. Searching the rest of the apartment, the officers discovered a severed head in the refrigerator, numerous photographs of dismembered murder victims, and various body parts, including severed heads, hands, and penises. There were also several corpses stored in acid-filled vats and implements presumably for use in constructing an altar, including candles, human bones, and skulls.

Dahmer was originally indicted on seventeen counts of murder, but that number was eventually reduced to fifteen. His trial began in January 1992. Confronted with overwhelming evidence against him, he pled not guilty by reason of insanity, but the court found Jeffrey Dahmer both sane and guilty on all fifteen counts of murder and sentenced him to fifteen consecutive life terms in prison.

He began serving his time at the Columbia Correctional Institution in Portage, Wisconsin, but on November 28, 1994, while on work detail in the prison gym, he was severely beaten, with a bar from a weightlifting machine, by fellow inmate Christopher Scarver. Dahmer died from his injuries while being transported to the hospital in an ambulance. Strangely and perhaps fittingly, Jeffrey Lionel Dahmer was beaten to death in the same way that he murdered his first victim, Steven Hicks.

First Contact

In June of 2008, WISP was contacted by Twofour Broadcasting (which was filming episodes of the British docudrama

Conversations with a Serial Killer) about conducting a paranormal investigation on the former site of Jeffrey Dahmer's apartment building. Although the building had been demolished after Dahmer's conviction, the property remained vacant. We were informed that a paranormal investigation had never been tried at the site. We also learned that we would have access to one key piece of Dahmer's bloody history: the front door to his apartment.

After the apartment building was demolished, the property owner had kept the door as a bizarre memento of the murders. I was fascinated by the symbolism the door conjured in my subconscious. This was the door that Dahmer's victims entered but never exited. It was a simple door that became the entry for the souls of Dahmer's victims to pass into the next world.

We would be the first team ever to conduct an investigation of the property, an opportunity too intriguing to pass up, so, a week later, we gathered our gear and made the drive from northern Indiana to Milwaukee to search for the ghosts of Dahmer's victims … and the possibly malevolent ghost of Jeffrey Dahmer himself. As it turned out, this investigation was unlike any adventure the four members of WISP had ever experienced.

After we arrived in Milwaukee and checked into our hotel room, Sam raised his concerns about the hosts of *Conversations with a Serial Killer*, especially ex-cop and self-proclaimed American psychic Bobby Marchesso. The whole team was aware of the seemingly endless supply of British paranormal television programs that feature alleged psychics prancing around like psychotic kangaroos and claiming to be possessed by the spirits of the dead. I assured Sam and the rest of the team that I had already raised such concerns with the show's producers and had even had a lengthy discussion with Bobby Marchesso himself on the subject. Bobby had admitted to having these same concerns and assured me that he had a reputation (not to mention a career) to uphold. He added that he found such behavior as distasteful and damaging to the reputations of credible psychics as we did. He assured me that no such paranormal hijinks would take place during this investigation.

The Investigation Begins

When we arrived at the site of Dahmer's demolished apartment building, the first thing we noticed was that the vacant lot was completely surrounded by a twelve-foot-tall cyclone fence crowned with a spiral of barbed wire. It was obvious that the owner of the property didn't take kindly to uninvited guests. Standing on the sidewalk near the fence were Bobby Marchesso and his co-host, British journalist Julie MacDonald. Where Bobby's role was to make contact and converse with the dead, Julie MacDonald took on the roles of resident skeptic and devil's advocate.

Since WISP had never before performed a paranormal investigation under the eyes of a film crew, a psychic, and a skeptic, we had no good idea what to expect. If nothing else, we told ourselves, the adventure promised to be entertaining. After spending a few minutes chatting with Bobby and Julie (which was made all the more interesting by Julie's Scottish accent), we saw director Chris Williams coming around the corner. He asked us to move to the rear of the property and prepare our gear while they filmed the opening sequence with Bobby and Julie. Soon, WISP would be the very first team of paranormal investigators to set foot on the site where many of Jeffrey Dahmer's gruesome murders had taken place.

As twilight fell, we readied our minds and our gear and watched the director and his crew filming the co-hosts as they walked the outside perimeter of the fence. We also noticed that we were starting to attract quite a bit of attention from the locals, a few of whom approached us to ask what we were up to. After explaining that we were a team of paranormal investigators on the prowl for the ghosts of Jeffrey Dahmer and his victims, local interest blossomed into enchantment. We were besieged by questions about our ghostly mission and our previous adventures.

While we were answering numerous questions about our techniques (and a few inquiries as to whether or not we knew those *"Ghost Hunters* guys" on TV), three squad cars pulled into the alley behind us and a small army of police officers exited the vehicles. At that point, most of the locals (including a few that looked more than a tad shady) dispersed and went about their business. The sudden appearance of the police officers had us concerned as well, but for a different reason: were the officers going to prevent us from entering the property?

We watched as the show's director spoke with the officers. A few minutes later, he handed a folded piece of paper to one of the officers, then walked over to the fence surrounding the property and unlocked the padlock on the gate. As it turned out, the police had stopped by to make sure that none of the locals were giving us any trouble. None had, so content that we were reasonably safe, the officers went on their way.

As I strapped a digital audio recorder to my arm and my teammates readied their gear, Chris Williams slid the chain from the gate that had kept the outside world away from the crime scene for so many years. The gate to the dark and murderous world of Jeffrey Lionel Dahmer had been unlocked. With a mixture of excitement and foreboding, we stepped through and entered what might have been another world, a world that promised to be unlike anything we had ever experienced before. Things were about to get surreal.

Haunted Grounds

WISP's first order of business was to walk the perimeter of the property. The purpose of this was twofold: first, to get a handle on how the property felt and to see if we could sense any active or residual energy patterns; and, second, to create an energy barrier (similar to what a group of Witches might do when creating sacred space) to keep any unwanted entities away from the property. We also wanted to keep any entities we summoned contained within our boundaries.

If the ghosts of Jeffrey Dahmer and his victims did prowl the grounds, we didn't want them vanishing into the night before we had a chance to interact with them. Our barrier would, we hoped, keep the ghosts contained. While we were walking the property line and building our magical barrier, the film crew was inside a large enclosed canopy that had previously been set up near the center of the property. They were busy setting up their cameras and audio recording gear. Inside the canopy was where we would perform the main components of our investigation and attempt to make contact with the dead.

As we walked, Amber came to an area of the property that she called a "natural doorway." It was through this invisible doorway that she believed paranormal activity could freely flow. Each member of the WISP team took a turn experiencing the doorway and sharing our impressions with one another. The final consensus was that there were indeed energies flowing in and out of the doorway and that they were quite possibly paranormal in origin. We agreed that it was in everyone's best interest not to tamper with this doorway and to allow it to function normally and without interference, even though it could possibly render the energy barrier we had erected around the property useless.

As the rest of the team made their way toward the canopy, I lingered outside for a few moments. I still hadn't decided how I was going to play the investigation, whether or not I was going to play "good cop" or "bad cop" with the ghost of Jeffrey Dahmer. If I was going to play the role of the provocateur, I knew that I would have to go all out, balls to the wall. I'd have to be a real son of a bitch.

My other option was to lie back and not stir the cauldron unless the situation required stirring up. Reflecting on the life of Dahmer and his criminal rampage brought me to a decision though, and, smiling a satisfied smile, I started walking toward the canopy where the film crew was waiting. As I approached to within thirty feet, I saw that director Chris Williams was locking the gate from the inside. As I took another step, someone spoke in my ear. I stopped in my tracks and looked around. No one was there. Everyone except Chris and I was inside the canopy. The voice I heard was decidedly female. I quickly reached for my audio recorder and scanned back. Had I captured the voice on audio? Hitting the play button, my question was answered. My smile grew even wider. I went inside the canopy to rejoin my teammates.

Doorway to the Otherworld

Inside the canopy was the aforementioned door to Apartment 213. The door was lying horizontally across two sawhorses. Sitting on the door were a small electric lantern, a pendulum hanging from a wooden stand, and a K2 meter, all of which belonged to Bobby Marchesso. I was very happy to see the K2 meter, as we had recently been considering purchasing one. This would be the perfect chance to try the device out and see if we were satisfied with how it performed.

The K2 meter was originally designed to be an electromagnetic field (EMF) detector that uses a series of colored lights to alert paranormal investigators to the presence of electromagnetic fields. It differs from standard EMF detectors that use a needle gauge or digital faceplate to show EMF levels. It was discovered by accident that the K2 meter is capable of eliciting yes and no answers from ghosts to questions being posed by paranormal investigators. The K2 meter works when an investigator asks a resident ghost a question that can be answered yes or no. Typically, the ghost is asked to light up the meter once for a yes answer and twice if the answer is no. We have often wondered if the K2 meter was also capable of detecting the energy we typically raise as a team prior to and/or during our investigations. The presence of this fascinating device would, we hoped, allow us to answer this question.

With the K2 meter in place and our digital audio recorders all functioning normally, the four members of WISP gathered in a circle around the door with Bobby Marchesso and Julie MacDonald. As usual, our first order of business was to raise energy as a group. The group energy-raising differs from the energy barrier we had put into place earlier while walking the perimeter of the property. It was now our intention to raise energy and use the door on the sawhorses as a metaphysical tool to open wide the doorway between the worlds of the living and the dead.

Bobby explained to us that Julie had previously had a very bad experience with energy work. He asked us to provide more detail on our procedures so Julie could determine whether she wanted to be involved in the energy-raising or sit it out. Amber gave an impressive and detailed account of how we did things and what to expect, and after consideration Julie decided that she would like to be involved. Amber also told Julie that if at any time during the energy-raising she started to feel uncomfortable, she could simply step away from the circle and we would quickly reconnect our circle and protect Julie from influences she wanted to avoid. Bobby, on the other hand, told us that he was a Reiki master and well versed in energy work. He already knew what to expect.

The six of us stood in a circle, took hands, and centered our bodies and minds. The energy began to flow freely, hurtling around us in our little circle. I noticed that Bobby was focusing on the door in the middle of the circle. Looking down at it, I instantly understood why. As the energy passed in front of the K2 meter, the device lit up and then went dark again when the energy passed behind it. This pattern continued the entire time we were raising energy. The answer to whether or not the meter was capable of picking up on our energy pattern was undeniable. But was the meter also capable of detecting and interacting with the dead? We were about to find out.

Our group continued to raise energy. We were delighted to see that Julie was handling things pretty well. In fact, at no time during the energy-raising did we feel any discomfort or blockage coming from her. Once the energy reached its height, I instructed our group to focus it into me. Once I felt the energy enter into me, I sent it directly into the door, using my ritual knife to direct it. As I did this, the lights of the K2 meter peaked at full and remained lit for well over fifteen seconds. I laid my knife on the door next to the other items to seal the circle.

With the job of containing the area and opening a doorway between the worlds accomplished, Bobby immediately informed us that he was already able to "sense a couple of Dahmer's victims." He added, "Dahmer is standing over in the corner of the canopy." Bobby further claimed that the ghost of Jeffrey Dahmer had been in our presence ever since we had taken our places around the door, but this was a claim that had yet to be proven to Julie and the four members of the WISP team.

Bobby then stated that if we wanted to "provoke or invoke" Dahmer's ghost in an attempt to trigger a physical response that could be recorded, now might be a good time to do so. Without hesitation, I asked, "Is there anyone here with us tonight? If so, can you speak to us? Can you make a noise? Can you move something in a non-harmful way?" Then Amber asked, "Why are you here?" Nothing. No audible response to our questions. The K2 meter was dark.

But things were about to change. Bobby informed us that more of Dahmer's victims had entered the canopy and that

Dahmer himself was moving around from corner to corner. Desperate to learn for sure whether or not these ghosts were in fact in our presence, I decided it was time to do some serious provoking. I would be satisfied with nothing less than hard evidence to back up Bobby Marchesso's claims. As the other members of the WISP team asked the ghosts questions in quiet, calm voices, I was getting more boisterous by the second. In fact, the more I thought about Jeffrey Dahmer and the monstrous things he had done when he was alive, the more pissed off I was getting. My boisterousness quickly blossomed into near rage.

"Is that true, Jeffrey?" I asked. "Are you here? Why don't you show yourself?"

Bobby then said that Dahmer's ghost had moved away from me and appeared to be frightened. Well, that was just fine by me. I continued my provocation.

"Why are you moving away from me, Jeffrey?" I demanded. "Is it because you're a coward? I think it's because you're a coward," I shouted. "I don't think you'll show yourself to me, and I don't think you'll speak to me." I continued, "I don't think you'll do anything. You're a fucking coward, Dahmer! I'm standing right here, and I'm not leaving without answers. Speak! Show yourself! If you're here, show us you're here!"

At that moment an unseen force brushed up hard against Amber's back, and she felt what she described as someone running their fingers through her hair. Had my provoking elicited a physical response? Or were the ghosts simply drawn to my teammate? Before any of these questions could be answered, one of the ghosts grasped Becca lightly by the arm, then let go. I watched in amazement as Bobby was able to point to the ghosts of Jeffrey Dahmer and his victims as they moved around inside the canopy, touching my teammates.

When Bobby said one of the ghosts had moved to Amber's right side, she felt an unseen force touch her on her right arm. When Bobby claimed that one of the ghosts was standing behind Becca, she felt something brush against her back. Even our resident skeptic, Sam, felt some unseen force touch him on the arm. Ever the sly investigator, Sam asked Bobby if one of the ghosts was standing near him, and if so, on which side. Impressively, Bobby was able to pinpoint a ghost standing next to Sam on the same side of his body where he had been touched. In a matter of minutes, it seemed that every one of us had experienced physical touching by the ghosts. Everyone, that is, but me.

Hot for a physical response from the ghost of Dahmer that could be recorded on film, I continued to shout at him. With all of the activity inside the canopy, however, I decided it might be better to tone things down a bit, so in a softer, more understanding voice, I asked, "Are you remorseful at all? Do you feel that you deserve any kind of punishment beyond what you've already received for what you've done to these people?"

My question triggered a response that Bobby claimed to see and hear, a response that our resident psychic found quite interesting. Bobby claimed that the question I posed triggered the following response from Dahmer's ghost: "I'll pay in more ways than you'll ever know."

Now Sam had a question, one that had been on my mind as well. Sam asked Dahmer if he was bound to the property or if he had come back because we were here. Bobby said that Dahmer's response indicated that he believed his ghost had returned to the property because of our presence. We all agreed with this. Becca wanted to know why Dahmer had done such unspeakable things while he was alive. Bobby claimed that Dahmer's response was that he "didn't know why," but Bobby also immediately stated that the response was a cop-out. He believed that Dahmer knew exactly why he had tortured and killed people, but he was reluctant to admit it in our presence.

The questions and answers continued until it became apparent that Bobby was becoming agitated by Dahmer's ghost. Bobby instructed Dahmer to quit "beating around the bush," and that it was time to "get past all of the bullshit." At that point, Julie asked Bobby if he could provide definitive proof that the ghost of Jeffrey Dahmer was in our presence. Bobby's response was that (I'm paraphrasing here) all he could do was relay his psychic impressions and that he couldn't "force" Dahmer's ghost to materialize in front of us. Julie continued by telling Bobby, "It's all very well when you're psychic to have a conversation with a ghost, but what we need is something physical. We don't need him just retelling the story. I could read a book for that. We need something additional."

Julie's impatience with the question-and-answer session was obviously getting under Bobby's skin, and he told his co-host to "ease up." He said, "The only way that I can do this is psychically." Now Amber spoke up, asking, "Jeffrey, is there anything you can tell Bobby about the murders that no one else could possibly know about?" By asking this question, Amber hoped to learn if Bobby Marchesso was really conversing with a dead serial killer or if the whole thing was one big put-on.

Julie and team WISP looked at Bobby in anticipation of an answer. It didn't take long to come. Without hesitation, Bobby informed us that Dahmer had killed two more people that no one but the murderer himself had known about. "The total number of people he killed was nineteen, not seventeen," Bobby said.

"Have they been found?" I asked.

"One was," Bobby said. "The body was found in a garbage dump, but the second body was never found."

I then asked Bobby if he could sense whether, in fact, these unknown murders had actually taken place, and if he could give us an idea of when. Bobby said he could and began going through the timeline of the Dahmer murders in his head. After some thought, he said he believed the unknown murders had taken place in May or June during the last year of Dahmer's bloody career. It was at that point that Bobby also stated that Dahmer's ghost had moved directly behind Amber and was peering over her left shoulder. Bobby believed that Dahmer had moved closer to Amber because he could sense compassion coming from her, but Amber later told us that her compassion was for the victims, not the murderer himself.

"Are you drawn to that compassion, Jeffrey?" I asked, and Becca immediately said, "Jeffrey, give us a sign. A sign that shows you're remorseful for what you've done."

"Earlier," I said, "someone lightly brushed by Amber's hair. Can you do the same thing? Can you give her a light touch on the shoulder or the arm?"

Two seconds later something touched Amber's arm.

Dahmer's ghost seemed much more interested in interacting with the people who had come to pay him a visit than the scientific and metaphysical gadgetry we had brought with us, though shortly after Amber was touched, Julie noticed that the pendulum was swinging back and forth in a regular pattern. Julie also told us that the pendulum had been moving since we'd begun our investigation. It wasn't until the pendulum had started swinging regularly, however, that she felt it was important to inform the rest of us. She then suggested that I should continue provoking the ghosts and trying to trigger a physical response. Bobby added that Dahmer's ghost was moving around inside the canopy and that he could direct me to him so I could get up close and personal.

I continued my provocation, following Dahmer closely at Bobby's direction, but every time I confronted him, he moved away from me. Bobby told me I reminded Dahmer of a cop he'd encountered while he was alive.

"I'm a paranormal cop," I replied.

At this point, I picked up my ritual knife from its resting place on the door and sheathed it. I did this because I felt there was a strong possibility that the powerful energy stored in the knife was keeping the ghosts from interacting with the other items on the door. Then, concerned that it could possibly be my own energy that was preventing Dahmer and the other ghosts from interacting with the equipment, I stepped outside the canopy. A few minutes later I went back inside and asked if my leaving had changed anything. The group's collective answer was no.

We were unable to trigger a response from the ghosts beyond light, physical touching and the gentle swinging of the pendulum. Now it was time for Bobby to do his thing. As the title of the TV series suggests, it was time for him to have a conversation with a dead serial killer.

A Conversation With a Serial Killer

Bobby wanted to go back and touch on the earlier comments Amber and Becca had made about Dahmer's lack of compassion for his victims. He believed that Dahmer's ghost was arguing with that assumption and denying it. Paraphrasing what Dahmer was telling him, Bobby said that Dahmer had "put great care into how he cut his victims and displayed them." Bobby claimed that the way in which Dahmer had displayed the severed heads and limbs of his victims had been done with compassion. Bobby further claimed that Dahmer had actually loved his victims, or, at least, "what he conceived as love."

I then asked Bobby if Dahmer considered the way in which he murdered and displayed his victims to be "art." Bobby nodded and said that Dahmer felt some of the things he had done with the bones and flesh of his victims was in fact a form of art. Amber wanted to know why Dahmer ate his victims, and Bobby replied that Dahmer's response was that "he was curious."

Now Bobby asked us to "hang on for a second." He paused for a few moments, sensing the energy patterns around him and listening intently to a disembodied voice that only he could hear. "When he says that he was 'curious,'" Bobby continued, "then I just feel like his mind is in a state of euphoria, but not a mental high caused by ecstasy, but, you know, like if a person's mind was under the influence of too much Demerol, you know what I mean? Too much codeine or a drug that gives a person an intense sensation of euphoria."

"Was he drunk when he was doing these things?" Julie asked.

"No," Bobby answered. "He ... um, he would fake drinking."

"Fake drinking? What do you mean, exactly?"

"When he would invite his victims over to his apartment to drink, he would, like, stick his tongue in the opening of the beer can and pretend to drink, but he wanted to be awake and alert for what was coming, so he wouldn't consume alcohol before or during the murders."

Although this assertion flew in the face of what is known about Jeffrey Dahmer, who in life was a chronic alcoholic, faking drinking so he would be alert prior to committing murder wasn't beyond the realm of possibility.

Now Sam wanted to return to the subject of Dahmer's unknown victims and glean a little more information. "There were more than seventeen victims, correct?" Sam asked.

"Yes," Bobby replied. "There were nineteen victims."

"And one of the victims wasn't found," Sam continued. "Can he tell us where any evidence of these murders might be found?"

"I don't think you're going to find any evidence," Bobby said. "I just got that psychically. It isn't something Jeffrey told me. Where he put one of the bodies was only a few blocks from here, and he didn't carve it up or do anything special to the body for whatever reason. I don't know if it was contaminated, which is the feeling Jeffrey is giving me. It almost feels like that victim had cancer or AIDS or something else that made the body contaminated."

"Was purity important to him in his victims?" I asked.

"Yes. Physical purity was important to him. In one of the places here in Milwaukee that we [meaning Bobby, Julie, and the Twofour crew] visited last night, a place Jeffrey was known to frequent when he was looking for victims, many of the people in there were strung out on drugs. They were desperate and full of sorrow, and Jeffrey's victims had to be above that kind of thing, you know? They had to be clean. His victims had to be above that sort of thing. They had to be cleaner and possess a sense of pride, and they also had to feel good about themselves. Or at least have that type of attitude."

"Did that increase his high when he killed them?" I asked. "Did victims full of pride increase Dahmer's euphoria?"

"Yes," Bobby replied. "He says yes."

Becca spoke up. "If he could say something to his parents," she said, "what would that be?"

"He's very, very apologetic," Bobby answered. "Very apologetic to his mom."

"What about his dad?" I asked.

"It feels like he's too ashamed of what he did to say anything to his dad," Bobby answered. "It feels like it's much harder for him to 'man up,' like, you know, the relationship between a boy and his father is a tougher thing to face. He's too ashamed to face him, even though his dad stood by him every step of the way, even after Jeffrey had been accused of the murders."

"I understand that you're only answering the questions we're asking," I said, "but I feel like we're almost humanizing him in a way. How does he perceive that? Do you get the feeling he's attempting to do that? Is he trying to put a mask over the monster?"

"I'm just bringing through what he's projecting," Bobby answered. "And I think throughout the entire investigation I've never felt 'monster.' It's different from our previous investigations where there was definitely an evil presence there, but this is something else. It's like with Jeffrey it's a switch, on-and-off kind of thing. I'm just not feeling *monster* is the correct word," Bobby said, turning his attention to the cameras and the film crew.

"I'm sorry," Julie interrupted, "but I disagree with that. You can't chop up seventeen people and stuff them into a bin in your house and not be a monster. I just disagree." She continued, "I just don't buy it. He did terrible things. And I understand how his mum and dad would feel: yes, they lost a son, but seventeen people lost their lives here. And, you know, why did you eat your victims? Because you were 'curious'? I just … I just find that astounding."

She turned to face Bobby directly. "You know, Bobby, something you and I have discussed is the parallel universe that Dahmer seemed to create for himself, where I can imagine those words being used quite genuinely in *his* world, to *love* someone, to be *curious* about someone, but to the rest of us that just seems completely ridiculous."

Bobby nodded his head. "Oh, of course," he agreed, "because society has one set of values and the people who do horrible things just don't see things the same way. So it's going to be very easy to label him as a monster because of what he did, the *horrific* things he did, but through *his* eyes, there is no, well, there was a right and wrong but—"

"Bobby," Sam broke in, "you said that he turned on and off like a switch. Are you saying, like, two separate personalities?"

Bobby nodded again. "I've come across dual personalities before, and this feels different from that, but it feels like [earlier in the evening] when we were talking about urges where if you have a habit, like a drug habit, an addiction, and you don't get what you need, it starts building up inside of you, and in Dahmer's case, his addictions led him to go through with it. With murder, I mean."

Amber had a question. "If Dahmer says it's *love*, then I wonder how he would have felt if someone had done such terrible things to him?"

Bobby's response was immediate. "He would have given himself freely." He paused for a moment, as if listening to a voice none of us could hear. "To be honest with you, I don't buy that answer. Even though he's telling me that, when I look at it from my rational mind, I'm like, no, you wouldn't have."

Now Becca spoke. "Obviously, when he was a child, his parents would have shown him what love really is—"

"He just moved over by you," Bobby put in, but Becca didn't acknowledge this.

"As a child," she continued, "how could he have distorted that, and then later on do the things he did and think it's love?"

I turned to Becca. "How do you know he was shown love as a child?" I asked. "You're making an assumption that he was shown that kind of love as a child. Do we know that for certain?"

"According to everything I've read about the Dahmer case," she replied, "his father, in particular, stood by him the entire time, even after he'd been arrested and accused of the murders."

Bobby said, "We [the film crew and the two hosts] have already visited the house he grew up in, and I felt a lot of abandonment there. I recall coming across factual stories about how his mother would leave him alone for long periods of time. When I was in the house, I also got the feeling that the abandonment played a part in why he started killing things, animals at first and then people later on. I also sensed that at one point he was sitting on the back porch of his house holding a skull in his hands and he was afraid to bury it. Imagine … like burying your pet. In his mind, burying his victims was adding a finality to things, like, 'I would have to let this go,' and he didn't want to do that. He felt like it was another form of abandonment, that if he buried them it would be like one more person leaving his life. That's why he took pictures of his victims. So he'd always have them with him."

Bobby paused and looked up. "He's bowing his head. And when I'm looking at that, at him bowing his head, it's coming across as a remorseful gesture. But I can't tell if it's an act, because now I'm looking at it from my perception. I've come out of Dahmer's head. I'm out, and now that I'm watching it, I don't know if I believe it. I question the depth of his apologies. I know I've felt his remorse a couple of times, but as I'm looking at this now, I don't know, he doesn't feel hugely remorseful."

Now Sam said, "To show remorse, he would have had to know the difference between right and wrong, wouldn't he?"

"He did know the difference," Bobby answered.

"And he did it anyway," Amber added.

"He did it anyway," Bobby agreed.

"So it was a choice," I said. "He wasn't sociopathic."

"It was a choice," Bobby agreed.

"So this brings us back to one of our original questions," Amber said. "Why did he do it? Did he want fame? The recognition that other people weren't giving him?"

"No," Bobby answered. He was quiet a minute, then said, "Control. He wanted control. There was a point when he was hunting, stalking, those sorts of things, and that's where the exoticness and the excitement came for him. It was only at the point when he drugged his victims and they started losing willpower that he started to relax. Then he was in total control and became very calm at that point. He could just do what he wanted to do at that point."

"Did he enjoy that aspect?" I asked. "Being the hunter?"

"Oh, yes," Bobby answered.

"There was chaos there," Amber said.

"Even danger," I added.

"Danger," Bobby said and nodded his head in agreement. "He was drawn to it."

"Well, that would tell me that he was a weak individual," Sam said. "If he was a strong individual, he would have enjoyed seeing the fear that he was causing in his victims. Since he wasn't seeing that fear because his victims were drugged, then he was a very weak person."

"The high was in the hunt," I added. "He couldn't handle seeing it in his victims."

Bobby gave a sigh and said, "He doesn't want to be here anymore. He's moving away from us now. He's stepping back. Fading."

"That's just fine with me," I said. "I really don't want to be in his presence any longer either."

But Becca had one more question for Jeffrey Dahmer. "Wasn't he himself hunted in prison?"

"Was he hunted?" Bobby asked, to make sure he had heard the question correctly. Becca nodded.

"Hang on," Bobby said. "Jeff," he said to the air, "did you know that you were going to be killed?" He paused again. "His answer is yes. Two or three days beforehand, he knew it was going to happen."

"So if he knew he was going to be killed, did it make him nervous?" Becca asked.

"Um, no," Bobby answered. "I mean, I'm sensing a little nervousness there, but I think that's just a human reaction, but he says that death was going to bring him relief."

"Did he feel he deserved to die?" I asked.

Bobby nodded. "He says yes. But as he says that," he paused again, "I'm getting the feeling that he's just saying that to give us another impression that he was remorseful. I think he's just telling us what we want to hear."

At this point Bobby told us that something quite interesting had just happened. He informed us that for the first time during the investigation, the ghost of Jeffrey Dahmer had moved around the door and was standing right beside me. "It's very interesting that he's moved over to you," Bobby said to me, "because in the beginning of the investigation, he was so afraid of you and didn't want to confront you, but now he says he has to 'raise himself up spiritually,' whatever that means." Now Bobby stepped closer to me and said,

"He's about this tall." He held his hand just above my left shoulder. "But I'm not sure how tall he was in real life."

"I'm six foot three in bare feet," I said, and then turned toward where Bobby claimed Jeffrey Dahmer's ghost was standing. I reached out with all of my senses, trying to pick up on a ghostly energy pattern. I could feel a presence standing near me, but not the kind of presence that I would expect to emanate from a dead serial killer.

Bobby said, "He still feels like he's trying to prey on compassion. He's hoping for some compassion from you, Marcus."

Bobby's words made me smile. "He's poking around in the wrong neighborhood if he's expecting compassion from me," I said.

"I'm done," Bobby said. "I'm done with the bullshit he's trying to feed us. I don't want to talk to him anymore."

At that point, I sensed the energy patterns inside the canopy beginning to change. I no longer felt a ghostly presence of any kind. Bobby acknowledged that the ghosts of Jeffrey Dahmer and his victims had departed through the unseen doorway we had created at the beginning of the investigation. Bobby then asked us if we wanted to close the circle of energy we had created inside the canopy. The four members of WISP agreed that it was time to do just that.

The six of us once again joined hands. We centered our bodies and our minds and concentrated on the circle of energy. "Thank you for being here," Becca said, speaking to the ghosts that had paid us a visit. "For your presence," she continued.

"Thank you for being gentle with us," I added. "Thank you for no harm."

"Thank you for your voices," Amber said. "For speaking to us."

"Sam," I asked, "do you want to seal the opening of the doorway for us?"

He nodded and without words began sealing the doorway by raising the circle of energy above us and compressing it into a ball. "Even after we have left this place," he said, "we leave behind our protection. Nothing may remain here that doesn't belong here. Nothing may remain that wasn't here all along. Nothing comes along with us. Everything stays. Our will. Our way."

Now Sam told us to concentrate on raising the ball of energy even higher above us. As a group, we compressed the energy tighter and tighter until we could feel it floating away from us, and Sam sent the energy away into the ether. It rose even higher, dissipating as it returned to its source. I placed my hand on the door to Apartment 213 one last time, and we all stood in silence, saying our unspoken goodbyes to the ghosts of the past, a past that will forever remain cloaked in darkness, due to some of the most horrific crimes in American history.

Leaving the Past in Peace

Upon exiting the canopy, there was much chatter about the investigation and what we had experienced. Bobby said that during the investigation he had felt a parallel between Dahmer and the fictitious character Hannibal Lecter, from the film and novel *The Silence of the Lambs*. Bobby believed that Dahmer had become so adept at hiding the monster inside him that if a person didn't know who and what he was, they would feel a sense of comfort in his presence.

Bobby's theory is supported by factual information. It is a well-known fact that after Dahmer had been arrested for the murders, several of the police officers in charge of overseeing him had actually come to like him a great deal. This is a phenomenon that even the officers themselves couldn't explain. I felt that the parallel between Jeffrey Dahmer and Hannibal Lecter was uncanny. Both men were connoisseurs and considered themselves to be artists. Both enjoyed the finer things in life. Both murdered and ate their victims.

As the rest of the group exited the property, I walked away from them. I had one last piece of unfinished business that I wanted to see to before I left. Earlier in the evening, before the investigation had begun, one of the locals had pointed out a small pile of bricks that was resting just inside the fence. These bricks were the last remnants of Jeffrey Dahmer's apartment building. I wanted to take one along as a souvenir.

Kneeling down and searching through the weeds and tall grass, I found what I was looking for, and then, with my paranormal prize in hand, I rejoined my teammates outside the gate. We snapped a few photographs with Bobby, Julie, and the film crew, then said our goodbyes and left the ghosts of Jeffrey Lionel Dahmer and his victims to their fate.

The Evidence

Before we begin to examine the evidence WISP collected during the investigation, there are there are a few things we should discuss, not the least of which is how different the investigation of Jeffrey Dahmer was from most of WISP's previous investigations. First was the presence of the film crew. I would like to start by mentioning their professionalism. The

Twofour crew are to be commended for their performance during the investigation. They were courteous to a fault and their work was seamless. The director and his crew were professional in every possible way.

The second thing that made the Dahmer investigation very different from our usual investigations was working with psychic Bobby Marchesso. Bobby and his co-host, Julie MacDonald, were also very friendly and very professional. It was also apparent to us that Bobby had his act together and was a pretty smart cookie. What is not apparent is whether or not Bobby was actually conversing with the ghost of Jeffrey Dahmer, as he had claimed. As I have said many times, I believe that there is only a small handful of psychics inhabiting our planet that possess such an extreme gift as being able to converse with the dead. Is Bobby Marchesso one of them? Well, only he knows for sure. But as the old saying goes, the proof is in the pudding, so without further delay let's take a look at the evidence. Let us decide for ourselves whether or not the ghost of Jeffrey Dahmer still prowls the ground in Milwaukee, Wisconsin.

Photographic evidence: WISP was unable to capture any evidence of paranormal activity on camera or camcorder during the investigation. This also holds true for the footage shot by the Twofour film crew.

Dahmer EVP in Chronological Order of Their Capture

Multiple EVP were captured on WISP's digital recorders during the investigation. Surprisingly, many of the voices captured were female, countering psychic Bobby Marchesso's claims that the only ghosts present during filming were those of Jeffrey Dahmer and his victims. All of Dahmer's known victims were male. What follows are descriptions of the EVP in chronological order of their capture.

1. Female voice: "Locking us in." This voice was captured outside the tent while we were walking the perimeter of the property and occurred at the exact moment that Chris Williams was locking the gate, clearly demonstrating that the ghost was aware of our presence. This is an A-class EVP, and is hands down the clearest voice of an NBE (non-biological entity) WISP has captured to date. All other EVP were captured inside the canopy.

2. Male voice: "Do, do, do, Bobby." This particular EVP is very odd and sounds like tribal chanting or singing.

3. Female voice: "A curse."

4. Two voices. Male voice: "Dahmer." Female voice: "What the hell?"

5. Male voice: "Wake the dead."

6. Voice, gender indeterminate: "Answer me."

7. Female voices (an investigator is asking the ghosts if they can interact with items on the table). First voice: "No." Second voice: "Maybe."

8. Male voices (over the top of the investigator's voice). First voice: "Maybe you should just let them do it." Second voice: "Shut up, you old fuck."

9. Male and female voices (at the time of capture, the investigator is provoking the ghost of Dahmer to speak and to show himself). Investigator: "Speak!"

Disembodied voice: "No." Investigator: "Show your-self." Disembodied voice: "No, no, no!" Investigator: "If you're here, show me you're here." Disembodied voice: "Noooo!" A female voice is then captured that cries out, "He can't do that!" Directly after these voices were captured, one of WISP's investigators was touched by an unseen entity.

Conclusion

Some compelling personal experiences and audio evidence gathered during the investigation reinforce the psychic's claims that ghosts were present at the location of Dahmer's former apartment building. However, the evidence is incon-clusive as to whether or not the paranormal activity was caused by the ghosts of Dahmer and his victims. Because di-rect responses to the investigators' questions prove that the entities were aware of our presence, the majority of para-normal activity would be considered intelligent rather than residual. The large number of female voices captured on digital recorders during the investigation is somewhat per-plexing, however, because the psychic claimed that only the ghosts of Jeffrey Dahmer and his victims were present at the scene. All of Dahmer's known victims were male.

After reviewing all of the evidence, WISP concludes that at the time of the investigation there were a large number of intelligent, self-aware entities present on the site. An un-seen force touched three of the four investigators during the investigation, but the touching is considered unsubstantiated reporting. There is no hard evidence to back up these claims, and they cannot therefore be considered as proof. On a personal note, however, I will mention that if members of my team state that they were touched, well, to me, their word is as good as gold. Nevertheless, without scientific evidence to back up these claims, I cannot in good conscience list the touching as hard evidence.

Beyond the EVP collected during the investigation and the personal experiences of my teammates, there was a significant amount of activity picked up by the K2 meter and the pendulum. However, the K2 meter seemed only to register the energy we raised as a group, not the yes and no responses from the dead, which the device is intended to do. Still, the K2 meter is a fascinating tool that warrants further study, so I promptly ordered one after I returned home from Milwaukee to field test during future investigations.

Another key feature of the Dahmer investigation worth mentioning is the atmosphere. At no time during the investigation did the members of WISP experience a sensation of intense darkness or evil. It isn't too hard to imagine that being in the presence of Dahmer's ghost would be akin to being in the presence of Satan himself. But as we discovered while doing research and during the subsequent investigation, when he was alive Dahmer had a gift for hiding the evil lurking inside him and placing a mask squarely over the face of his inner monster. If Dahmer's ghost was in fact present during the investigation, it is obvious that he carried this gift with him to the grave.

All in all, the Jeffrey Dahmer investigation was another fascinating glimpse into the strange and often shadowy world of the paranormal. Strong and frequent paranormal activity occurred during the investigation.

Before I leave you to your own ghosts, there is one more piece of the paranormal puzzle I would like to share with you. This is one of the many strange EVP collected at the scene, the EVP in which a disembodied male voice says, "Shut up, you old fuck." This EVP is intriguing. Using the voice-analyzing software on my computer, I was able to isolate and enhance this voice, after which I Googled in search of video footage of Jeffrey Dahmer while he was still alive.

As it turned out, there was quite a bit of footage floating around on the Internet, most of which was filmed during Dahmer's trial. As soon as I heard Dahmer speak, a cold chill washed over me. I scanned back through the video, listening to it over and over again. *The voice I was hearing was a perfect match to the EVP in every way.* The two voices were identical. There is no doubt in my mind that WISP had captured the disembodied voice of Jeffrey Lionel Dahmer.

Chapter 6

State Road 124: Okie Pinokie and the Demon Pillar Pigs

Investigation: The Legend of Okie Pinokie

Start date: August 7, 2010

Place: Peru, Indiana

The Legend[7]

The area known as Okie Pinokie is a heavily wooded parcel of land located near the Mississinewa Reservoir outside of the city of Peru, Indiana. At the intersection of Indiana State Road 124 (locally known as the River Road) and County Road 510 E, three stained and timeworn concrete pillars mark the entrance to Okie Pinokie. Snaking through the woods are rough hiking trails that are mainly used by riders on horseback.

At one time the area was extremely swampy, and, according to Mississinewa staff, at least eight decaying human bodies have been discovered there. Local experts believe that the surrounding area was once used as a burial ground by nomadic tribes of Native Americans. Due to this information, locals

---

7. Research sources: GhostPlace.com (www.ghostplace.com) and the Indiana Ghost Hunters' website, specifically http://hoosierghost .proboards.com/index.cgi?board=discussion&action=print &thread=24.

have come to believe that thousands of Native American spirits dwell within the woods.

Legend states that as you drive down the gravel road that leads into Okie Pinokie, the trees and underbrush will swarm around your vehicle. If you make it past the trees, you will eventually come to a circular drive that marks the end of the road. If you get out of your car there and whistle, someone (or some*thing*) will whistle back at you from deep inside the forest.

There have been reports of people hearing the squealing of a pig near the pillars, but upon investigation no pig can be found. Legend also has it that a seven-year-old girl named Stephanie was tortured and murdered in Okie Pinokie, and that on certain nights you can still hear her screams and see her ghost wandering through the woods.

Investigating the Legend

We were warned never to use a Ouija board in Okie Pinokie, because the resident spirits don't like it and become upset. So naturally the first thing WISP did was go out and buy one. We found a really nifty Ouija board at our local Toys "R" Us store. It glows in the dark.

Testing the Ouija board in Okie Pinokie topped our list of experiments to perform during our investigation. But as usual, before a full investigation of Okie Pinokie could take place, we would have to research the legend and pay a daytime visit to the woods to get a clear idea of exactly what we were dealing with. Reports we had read stated that much of the terrain in Okie Pinokie is primitive and rough going. Plotting a course through the woods prior to our nighttime visit was therefore paramount to a safe and a successful investigation of the legend.

The road (and I use that word loosely) that leads into Okie Pinokie is rough gravel and appears to be more of a fire access lane than an actual roadway. The entrance is very difficult to find, and in the end we had to rely on our GPS navigation system to locate it. Sam and Amber were unavailable to help with the daytime investigation, so Becca and I decided to go it alone. If the two of us turned up anything promising, all four members of the WISP team would return to Okie Pinokie at a later date. As the road curved past the tree line, we kept a close watch for the phenomenon of the trees swarming around the vehicle. It never happened. I theorized that the tree swarming was nothing more than a visual illusion that occurred mainly at night.

About a mile and a half up the road, we reached the circular drive where the road abruptly ended. This was the spot where reports stated that the paranormal activity occurring in Okie Pinokie was the strongest. After strapping our digital recorders to our arms and readying our photographic equipment, Becca and I exited the vehicle.

About twenty yards from where we had parked, we saw a middle-aged couple who were loading two horses into a trailer attached to a pickup truck. The couple was looking at us rather suspiciously, so I gave them a nod and a smile. They returned my greeting and seemed to relax. After they finished loading their horses, Becca and I walked over to them to see if they would be willing to speak with us about the legend of Okie Pinokie. As it turned out, they were more than happy to tell us what they knew. After introducing ourselves and explaining that we were researching a book I was writing about local legends, the couple eagerly began spouting information. I thought it best to keep to ourselves the fact that we were ghost hunters (not to mention Witches), and I never once mentioned the subject to them.

The gentleman began speaking first, and informed us that "a lot of weird kids wearing trench coats come out here with Ouija boards and perform satanic rituals." He then pointed to a gully off to his left and said, "If you walk across that gully and up the trail on the other side, you'll find a bunch of stones with weird symbols those kids have painted on them." We'd read numerous accounts about young people frequenting Okie Pinokie after dark to make contact with ghosts, so the information about rituals being performed in the woods came as no surprise.

But what the man told us next caught our interest. After I told the couple that "most of these kids probably wouldn't know a ritual from a hole in the ground" and that "there was probably nothing to worry about," the look on the man's face became serious.

He looked me in the eyes and said, "Five years ago, I would have agreed with you, but those rocks I told you about? The ones up top of the trail? Well, every time we ride past them, the horses get really spooked like there's a predator around or something. I'm telling you, those kids are stirrin' up something that they shouldn't be messing around with."

The news of the spooked horses came as a surprise, and I started wondering if some of the kids who were performing the rituals might actually know what they were doing and had purposely awakened something in the woods.

After giving us clear directions to the ritual area, the couple started gathering up the rest of their belongings and prepared to leave. But before they did, there was one last thing I wanted to ask them about: the Hobbit house.

Somewhere deep inside the woods in Okie Pinokie is a structure approximately the size of a large doghouse that the locals often refer to as the *Hobbit house*. We had seen numerous photographs of the Hobbit house on the Internet. The photos show how the structure got its name. It is constructed of concrete blocks in the shape of a half circle, and looks very similar to the Hobbit houses in the *Lord of the Rings* films. The structure is (of course) reported to be haunted, and on many occasions has been used by local geocaching treasure hunters to store caches of goodies for their fellow hunters to find. This treasure-hunting game is similar to a game of hide and seek, but instead of seeking people, the participants conceal a stash of items somewhere and then post the coordinates on the Internet for their fellow treasure hunters to seek out. A logbook is commonly left with the cache so the hunt can be documented.

Even though the treasure hunting in Okie Pinokie seemed interesting, WISP was interested in a different kind of hunt altogether. The couple informed us that they knew where the Hobbit house was located, but they also told us that it was deep in the woods and that getting to it on foot would be difficult. I asked them for directions to the Hobbit house anyway, and they told us how to get there. As it turned out, the house was located quite a ways away from where we were parked. For the time being, Becca and I were much more interested in investigating the area surrounding the circular drive and locating the spot where the rituals had been taking place. We thanked the couple for their time and walked over to the edge of the gully to which the gentleman had directed us.

Sounds in the Woods

The embankment overlooking the gully was very steep and covered with a dense tangle of vegetation. We started wondering how the team would fare traversing the woods after dark. It was obvious that we would need to be outfitted with heavy clothing and hiking boots, plus a portable emergency medical kit. Before entering the gully, Becca and I checked our cell phones for a signal. The reception was weak, but we determined that we would be able to get a call out in case of an emergency.

As we made our way down into the gully and up the hiking trail on the other side, I stared getting a sense of how Okie Pinokie got its haunted reputation. We hadn't seen or heard anything unusual yet, but at the same time there was something about the woods that felt mysterious. The landscape seemed more like a mirage than a forest. It felt as though nature itself was consciously concealing something otherworldly in its midst. There was a presence here. Or perhaps a better word might be *intelligence.* Far below the hill where we were standing was a river, its water brown with mud. Recent rainfall in the area had also turned the hiking trails into quagmires. These muddy trails were another potential hazard we might have to deal with during our nighttime investigation. We had been in Okie Pinokie for less than forty-five minutes and the hardships of investigating the area were already becoming apparent to us. But for the time being, the hilltop was the perfect place to test one of Okie Pinokie's legends.

As I mentioned, one of the legends surrounding Okie Pinokie is that if you whistle in the woods, someone will whistle back to you. The most logical culprits responsible for the whistling should be living persons, not ghosts, as many reports claim. This isn't to say that I don't believe that ghosts aren't capable of making an audible response, but rather that an earthly explanation seemed much more likely than a paranormal one. But be that as it may, I decided to give it a try.

I'm a half-assed whistler at best, but I managed to get off a few good ones. There was no response. However, while I was testing the legend I discovered something quite interesting: sound waves don't travel very far in Okie Pinokie. This was unexpected. Apparently the makeup of the landscape causes sounds to fall flat. The peaks and valleys in Okie Pinokie simply don't allow for good acoustics. I also noticed that if Becca and I were more than fifteen feet apart, it was very difficult to make out what we were saying to each other. Exactly how (and if) the poor acoustical properties of the woods came into play with the legend remained unknown. During our nighttime investigation, WISP would do more extensive testing with sound, but there was still a considerable amount of ground for Becca and me to cover during our daytime visit. We still needed to locate the Hobbit house and the spot where the rituals had been taking place.

Mischief or Magic?

It took us well over an hour to locate the spot in the woods where the (allegedly satanic) rituals had been taking place, and by then we were running low on steam. The steep, muddy trails were taking their toll on our bodies and our willpower, but we knew that we had to find the motivation to keep going.

At first sight, the ritual area appeared to be well used and intelligently constructed. Large, fallen tree limbs had been lashed together in a square around the ritual area. It was obvious that campfires had been lit inside the ritual area in spite of the large sign near the entrance to Okie Pinokie that states that fire of any kind is prohibited in the forest. Such obvious disregard for fire safety made me wonder exactly what type of individuals had been performing the rituals. A seasoned magical practitioner would never, I told myself, put the forest and its inhabitants in jeopardy for the sake of a ritual fire. The thought of someone doing so angered me.

Encircling the ritual area were the painted rocks the couple had told us about. Closely inspecting the rocks and the symbols painted on them, I was instantly reminded of the ritual area we had discovered in Munchkinland during one of our earlier investigations. Like the chalk symbols we had discovered at Munchkinland, the symbols painted on these rocks seemed random and made no sense whatsoever. The symbols seemed to have no magical correspondence with each another. It looked like someone had brought a book on symbology to the ritual area and painted the rocks with the ones the participants thought looked the coolest. One of the rocks had been painted with an ankh and a swastika, another with an inverted pentagram and the astrological symbol for Taurus. These unrelated symbols made me think of a group of inept, wannabe magical practitioners trying to make contact with ghosts and instead summoning a satanic Taurean Nazi with a penchant for ancient Egypt.

Still, there was something about the ritual area that was unsettling. It gave Becca and me an uneasy feeling. We sensed an energy here that felt old and angry. We now understood why horses might become spooked while traveling too close to the stones. Becca and I agreed that investigating the ritual area as a full team was a must. As intriguing (not to mention mystifying) as the ritual area was, however, we would soon be running out of daylight and we still had to locate the Hobbit house. We were a good distance away from the van, and according to the directions we had been given, the Hobbit house was a few miles in the opposite direction from where we were parked. It was clearly time to keep moving.

As we made our way back toward the circular drive where the van was parked, Becca and I started hearing whispers in the woods. We looked around. There wasn't another living person in sight, and we had already determined that sound waves didn't travel far inside the woods. We couldn't account for the strange voices. As we walked, we began asking simple questions in hopes of capturing responses on our digital recorders. As we neared the gully we had crossed on our way to the ritual area, something unseen slapped Becca across her forehead. There was enough force behind the slap to make her cry out in pain. I tried to discuss what had happened with her, but she cut me off mid-sentence. "I no longer feel welcome in this part of the woods," she said. I took her by the hand, and we made our way across the gully and out of the woods.

Hobbits, Ghosts, and iPhones

As we neared the circular drive where the van was parked, we saw that Okie Pinokie was starting to get crowded. There were no fewer than three pickup trucks parked near the van and at least as many groups of riders on horseback nearby. As Becca stashed our photographic equipment inside the van, I walked over to one of the groups of riders to ask for clearer directions to the Hobbit house. The riders were more than happy to help, but one of the women in the group informed me that getting to the Hobbit house on foot would take us well over an hour. This wasn't good news. It was already late afternoon and attempting a two-hour round trip to the Hobbit house so late in the day was a bad idea. The rough terrain had already taken its toll on our bodies, and Becca and I were running low on energy and hydration.

After a short discussion, we decided to locate the trail that led to the Hobbit house but to save the actual trek for when we returned as a full team. At this point it was obvious that if there were any chance of WISP performing a full investigation, the team would have to return to Okie Pinokie early in the day and stay deep into the night. We also considered the possibility that we might have to make numerous trips to Okie Pinokie to be able to cover all of the spots we wanted to investigate. Armed with fresh directions and a clear idea of what we would be dealing with upon our return, Becca and I climbed into the van and went in search of the trail that led to the Hobbit house.

The woman on horseback had told me that the best way to find the trail we were looking for was to follow the road back the way we had come and look for a metal gate just off to the right side of the road. As we neared the turnoff that led to the gate and the trail beyond it, Becca demanded that I stop the van. She had seen something cross the road ahead of us, something she had no explanation for.

"What did you see?" I asked as I slowed the van and brought it to a stop along the side of the road. Looking ahead, I saw that we were within fifteen feet of the turnoff for the trail.

"I'm not sure," she said. "For lack of better words, it looked like air displacement."

"Air displacement? What do you mean?"

"You know," she began, "something moved across the road, but I couldn't quite make out what it was. It was like a shimmer of light moving through the air."

"Like in *Predator*?" I asked.

"Yes. Just like in *Predator*."

I was referring to the 1987 movie starring Arnold Schwarzenegger. In this movie, the Predator (an alien) has a cloaking device that mimics its surroundings to conceal itself from view. The cloak occasionally gives off a faint shimmer of light, a visual phenomenon that looks like displaced air.

While I'm not suggesting that Okie Pinokie is overrun with aliens, I theorized that a partially materialized ghost had created the visual phenomenon Becca had seen. Since we were parked so close to the turnoff for the trail to the Hobbit house, Becca decided to get out of the van and take some photographs to see if she could capture the phenomenon on camera. After she snapped a few shots, we walked up the road to the turnoff.

The woods surrounding the Hobbit trail felt different from the parts of Okie Pinokie we had investigated thus far. The area was quiet and serene, and yet we could sense an unseen presence. The woods here felt thick with the ghosts of the past. Just ahead of us at the top of a steep hill was the entrance to the trail we were looking for. As Becca lingered to take more photographs, I ventured up the hill to get a better look. Like the rest of Okie Pinokie, the Hobbit trail was thick with mud and, for the time being at least, all but impassable. When I rejoined Becca ten minutes later, I discovered that she was engaged in a rather unusual activity. She was tracking ghosts with her iPhone.

Everyone who knows Becca personally knows that she loves her gadgets. She has numerous applications installed on her iPhone, one of which is an app called Ghost Radar®. The creators of Ghost Radar® (an outfit called Spud Pickles) claim that their application is capable of detecting paranormal activity by using internal sensors located inside iPhones and other handheld electronic devices. What follows is a description of Ghost Radar® and how it works, taken directly from the Spud Pickles website:[8]

> *Ghost Radar is a portable application designed to detect paranormal activity … Ghost Radar attempts to detect paranormal activity by using various sensors on the device on which it is running. Like traditional paranormal detecting equipment, Ghost Radar employs sensors that measure electromagnetic fields, vibrations, and sounds. However, traditional paranormal equipment can be easily fooled when simple mundane bursts of normal electromagnetic fields, vibrations, and sounds occur. Ghost Radar sets itself apart by analyzing the readings from sensors giving indications only when interesting patterns in the readings have been made.*

---

8. www.spudpickles.com/.

Okay. Let's look at this logically. While an iPhone is almost certainly capable of detecting sounds and even vibrations, to me the thought of the device containing sensors capable of detecting electromagnetic fields was laughable. After I did a quick Internet search on my own iPhone, however, I discovered I was wrong. Apparently an iPhone's internal compass can be affected by electromagnetic fields. But even so, I was still having a hard time believing that a cell phone was capable of detecting paranormal activity. What happened next, however, threw my belief into question.

According to Becca's Ghost Radar®, there were three ghosts in our immediate vicinity. Looking in the direction where the radar was indicating activity, I saw the same shimmer of light that Becca had seen earlier. Around the shimmer I saw the visual phenomenon that she had referred to as "air displacement." But it was unlike anything I had ever seen before. The area in which the air displacement was occurring was well shaded. It was unlikely that it was being created by sunlight or heat waves rising from the ground. The shimmer quickly faded from view, and as it did, the Ghost Radar® "spoke" aloud four words: *crowd, close, moving,* and *dog.* Becca and I were fascinated. Less than a minute later, a large group of riders on horseback rounded the corner and came into view. Trailing behind the riders was a dog. A blue heeler, to be exact.

Beyond its ability to detect paranormal activity, the Ghost Radar® is also supposedly capable of picking up the disembodied voices of the dead and playing them back over the iPhone's speakers. After what Becca and I had just seen and heard, we were quickly becoming believers. Thus far, the Ghost Radar® had exhibited a precision that went far beyond anything we could chalk up to mere coincidence. There was obviously a paranormal intelligence at work here. But making further contact with the ghosts would have to wait until we could return as a full team. The sun was beginning to set, and without our flashlights and proper attire, Becca and I were ill prepared to conduct an after-hours investigation on our own. Leaving the ghosts of Okie Pinokie in peace, we made the long drive back home and began sifting through the evidence. What we had captured on our audio recorders was nothing short of amazing.

An overwhelming number of EVP were captured on audio recorders during our daytime investigation of Okie Pinokie. So overwhelming, in fact, that I will forego normal protocol and list the daytime EVP separately from the EVP WISP captured during our nighttime investigation. The following EVP are A-class and B-class, and are therefore suitable to submit as evidence. However, please note that many other potential EVP were captured during our daytime investigation that were either indeterminate or of too poor a quality to submit as evidence. Daytime EVP of the quality WISP was able to capture at Okie Pinokie are rare, and I hope you find them as fascinating as we do.

Okie Pinokie Daytime EVP in Chronological Order of Their Capture

- As Becca and I are walking through the gully, a disembodied female voice was captured that says, "Follow the channel."

- As I tell Becca that the Hobbit house is "back that way," a disembodied male voice asks, "Where?" Interestingly, a musical note sounds just as the voice begins to speak. The note is similar in sound and tone to what would be produced by a stringed instrument.

- The disembodied voice of a young male says the word, "Speak."

- As Becca repeats the words, "Testing, one, two, three," after experiencing a short-lived problem with her digital audio recorder, the hissing voice of a disembodied female says, "Stop."

- As I whistle in an attempt to elicit a response per the legend, a male voice clearly states, "I bet you someone's going to react to that." The tone of this voice is unique and unlike any voice WISP has captured to date. This voice sounds very close to the recorder's microphone and is (for lack of a better term) quite troll-like. Immediately after the voice is captured, I say, "I thought I just heard something."

- A ghostly voice says, "Wooooo." This voice sounds very close to where we were standing and was audible at the time of capture. In fact, Becca and I are heard mimicking the voice to determine whether or not we had both heard the same thing. We had.

- As Becca is complaining about mosquitoes and poison ivy, a disembodied female voice says, "I see a man in the rocks." A Southern drawl is evident in the voice, and at the time of capture I was standing among several large boulders.

- As I call out the word, "Hello?" a disembodied male voice replies, "Hi."

- As Becca sees the air-displacement phenomenon for the second time, a disembodied female voice says the words "sun" and "fly."

- As Becca is turning on the Ghost Radar® application on her iPhone (which she mistakenly refers to as the "Ghost Talker"), a female voice asks, "Does it talk?"

Stephanie: The Lost Girl of the Woods

Before returning to Okie Pinokie as a full team, WISP scoured the Internet in search of in-depth information about Stephanie, the lost girl of the woods. After countless hours of searching, we found little information beyond what we already knew. This information is (1) that a seven-year-old girl named Stephanie was allegedly tortured and murdered in Okie Pinokie, and (2) that on certain nights you can still hear her screams and see her ghost wandering through the woods.

Junior Investigator

At two o'clock in the afternoon on September 5, 2010, WISP headed for Okie Pinokie with a new team member, Becca's twenty-year-old son, Ryan. The night before the investigation, a powerful windstorm blew through the town in which I live, toppling an enormous tree in my yard and burying the WISP van under heavy branches. In an incredible stroke of luck, the van was undamaged, but it took Sam, Ryan, and me the entire morning to clear away the debris. Not a good start, considering that the investigation of Okie Pinokie promised to test the team's physical endurance.

After the tree was cleared, Ryan asked me if he could join us on the investigation as a favor in return for his help. Although I had resisted the idea of allowing anyone to join our investigations in the past, Ryan had been raised in a Pagan household and possessed a basic understanding of magic and how the team went about performing investigations. I had, in fact, been considering allowing him to join us on a hunt for some time. After a short discussion with Ryan about protocol, I agreed that he could join the team as we set out for Okie Pinokie.

Arrival

When we arrived at Okie Pinokie, the entire area was teeming with human activity. It was Labor Day weekend, and the trails and woods were full of riders on horseback. We had anticipated running into a holiday crowd, of course, and were counting on the activity settling down by nightfall. As we set up base camp at the edge of the circular drive, the team began attracting quite a bit of attention from the locals. We really couldn't blame them. Our base camp was extensive. We had brought along coolers packed with food and Gatorade and five camp chairs, plus three folding tables to accommodate our huge supply of scientific and metaphysical gadgetry.

Our base camp was so extensive, in fact, that it took us nearly two hours to set everything up, by which time only a few precious hours of daylight remained. We still had to perform a test run on our equipment and locate the Hobbit house.

Wanderers in the Woods

While Becca, Sam, and Ryan remained in the camp, Amber and I ventured into the woods in search of the Hobbit house.

We easily located the entrance to the trail, but much to our dismay we saw that the main path branched off in many different directions. Unlike the rest of Okie Pinokie, this part of the woods was devoid of human activity, and without guidance we would have to rely on our instincts to locate the Hobbit house—a task we quickly discovered was much easier said than done.

From our research, we knew that the Hobbit house was visible from the trail. But the spring and summer weather in northern Indiana had been hot and wet, and so the woods were overrun with a healthy growth of saplings and other vegetation. There was a very real possibility that Amber and I would walk right past the Hobbit house without seeing it. And that's exactly what happened. After well over an hour of hiking without sighting the Hobbit house, we were ready to abandon our search and concentrate our efforts on other parts of the legend, but by then we were very near the edge of the woods, so we decided to keep going until we reached the end of the trail. Haunted or not, the woods surrounding Okie Pinokie were indescribably gorgeous, and despite the physical exertion, Amber and I were thoroughly enjoying our hike.

After taking a short breather and performing some EVP work at the edge of the woods, we started back down the trail toward our base camp. As we walked, we kept a close watch for the Hobbit house. Ten minutes later we found it. Just as we had predicted, it was obscured from view by the dense growth, and it was only by chance that I noticed a shadowy patch in the woods that appeared too uniform to be natural. This was the entrance to the Hobbit house.

As we made our way through the woods, Amber and I expressed our delight that our efforts hadn't been in vain. We were so delighted, in fact, that as soon as we reached the Hobbit house we crawled inside, ignoring the fact that the small structure was crawling with spiders. As Amber and I huddled inside the Hobbit house, we could sense the lingering energy left behind by those who had come here before us. We could also sense an unseen presence in the woods, but we agreed that the sensations we were feeling could simply be the echoes of the legend of Okie Pinokie playing tricks on our subconscious. As happy as we were to sit inside the Hobbit house and ponder this question, however, we knew that we couldn't stay for long. The sunlight filtering down through the trees was growing dimmer, and we still had a long hike back to our base camp.

Leaving the Hobbit house, we marked the trail with arrows fashioned from fallen branches. We planned to return after nightfall, and these markers would be invaluable in finding our way through the woods after dark. But when we arrived back at camp, we discovered that, due to unpredictable circumstances, team WISP would be forced to alter all of its plans.

Ghost Hunters in Training

Amber and I immediately noticed that Sam and Becca were upset about something. They informed us that while we were in the woods, three teenage boys had driven up and parked nearby. Spying our equipment, the teenagers asked if they could participate in the investigation. Becca had told them that Amber and I were in the forest looking for the Hobbit house and that they would have to wait until we returned to get my permission to join the hunt. This was something that Becca knew I would be hesitant to do. Then Sam informed me that the teenagers were determined to investigate Okie Pinokie with or without our help and had returned to town to stock up on flashlights and bottled water. He was concerned that if I didn't allow the teenagers to accompany us, they might disrupt our investigation and possibly even play pranks on us. He also said that the teenagers seemed like "really nice kids." At that moment I knew that we would have to drastically alter our plans. There was no way around it.

But to everyone's surprise (including my own), I wasn't all that unhappy about the change of plans. Looking at Ryan (who was sitting at one of the tables fiddling around with his mother's Ghost Radar® app), I found myself secretly excited about leading a group of youngsters on a ghost hunt in Okie Pinokie. I recalled the summer nights of my own youth, and how my friends and I used to sneak into a graveyard late at night in hopes of seeing a ghost. Or to give each other a little scare. These recollections brought a big smile to my face. I also knew that if the kids ran into any trouble with the locals (something that I knew from reports I had read about Okie Pinokie was a very real possibility), there would be adults around to protect them.

As the sun began to set, the three boys (Rodney, Jordon, and Steve) returned, and I sat them down for a long talk about protocol and what my terms were for letting them join the hunt. I was specifically concerned about any audio and photographic evidence being contaminated. The boys understood that beyond my investigatory concerns I was also worried about safety. They promised to be respectful and obey my commands without question. After strapping audio recorders to the boys' arms and tying glow sticks to their belt loops so we could keep track of them in the dark, Amber, Ryan, and I led them into the woods, while Sam and Becca stayed at base camp to add live updates to Twitter and perform their own investigation. Leading this amateur team down the road and into the forest made me feel like a Scout leader leading his unsuspecting troops on a snipe hunt.

Ancients and Newbs

As we led the boys along the trail to the Hobbit house, Amber and I discovered that the two-way radio we had brought to keep in contact with base camp was all but useless. We were able to send and receive transmissions, but they were garbled and filled with static. Fortunately, however, the push-to-talk feature on Amber's cell phone was working just fine, and we were able to use it to contact Sam without any problems. The ability to communicate with base camp was essential in order to keep the investigation going. I wasn't about to lead a group of adolescents into the woods after nightfall without a way to summon help in case of an emergency.

We soon came to the first trail marker Amber and I had left earlier in the day. The marker was undisturbed, which was good news. It meant that the hunt could continue. As we walked along the trail, I couldn't help but notice that the forest was much creepier at night. It was pitch-black, and even our flashlights and glow sticks looked weak in the darkness surrounding us. The haunting calls of owls and night birds filled the woods, and I wondered if the birdcalls weren't in some small part responsible for the legend of Okie Pinokie. Many of the calls sounded like moans and screams. From far in the distance came the echoing voices of some of the locals who had stayed in the area past nightfall. I reminded the team to note any human sounds they heard on their voice recorders so I wouldn't mistake them for EVP while going over the evidence.

We came to our second trail marker, and then the third. We were very close to the Hobbit house now. Off to our right, we saw a strange glow of green light emanating from the woods. It was very close to the Hobbit house. As we left the trail, we discovered that the green glow was coming from the ground directly in front of the Hobbit house. Amber and I quickly deduced that it was caused by phosphorus paint or some other manmade substance that had been spilled or purposely poured on the ground. There was nothing paranormal about the glow whatsoever. That's when we started wondering if the legend of Okie Pinokie was nothing more than an elaborate hoax. But hoax or otherwise, we still had an investigation to perform.

While Amber shot video of the area, I scanned the inside of the Hobbit house with my flashlight. The number of spiders clinging to the walls and ceiling had tripled, and I wasn't about to enter the house a second time. As I knelt before it, Rodney, the oldest of the three boys, told us an interesting story he had heard from one of his friends. Rodney's friend had told him that he had visited the Hobbit house himself, and that upon investigation he had found a handwritten note inside it. The note, which had been rolled, tied with a red string, and stuck inside a glass jar, read as follows: *Congratula-*

tions! You have found the Hell Hut. Stand on top of the Hell Hut and follow the path of illumination.

The phosphorus paint now made sense. I asked Rodney to follow the instructions written on the note. He easily climbed up on top of the four-foot-tall structure and scanned the area with his flashlight. I snapped a series of photos with my still camera at the same time, and as the flash from my camera lit up the woods, I saw pinpoints of light coming from the trees. At first, I thought the lights were the eyes of forest creatures such as squirrels or raccoons. But I was wrong. As I walked over to one of the trees from which the flashes of light had come, I saw that a series of large nails had been pounded into the tree trunks, and the heads of the nails had been coated with reflective paint. *Follow the path of illumination*, I thought. All of this was obviously the work of pranksters or treasure hunters. I could sense no paranormal activity occurring in the area.

But that was about to change.

While Ryan stood near the Hobbit house testing his mother's Ghost Radar®, I tested what I considered to be the most unlikely part of the legend of Okie Pinokie. This was the legend of Stephanie. When I gave a loud whistle, I instantly noticed that sound waves traveled much farther in Okie Pinokie after dark than they had during our daytime investigation. There was no response to my whistling. "Stephanie," I called out, "Stephanie. Are you here?" Not a sound. No response of any kind.

I was about to call off the investigation due to lack of activity, when all at once we could hear whispering and footfalls all around us. The sounds were very close. I clicked on my flashlight and shone it around the house. The four boys did the same. The sounds ceased. There was no one there. I instructed the boys to kill their flashlights, which they did without hesitation.

As soon as our lights went dark, the whispered voices and sounds of footfalls resumed. I started asking simple questions in hopes of catching a response on my audio recorder as Amber shot video with her camcorder, which Sam had outfitted with a bank of powerful infrared lights. If anything paranormal appeared, she was certain to catch it on video. Ryan then announced that his Ghost Radar® was showing three paranormal entities close by. I discounted this information until the Ghost Radar® began "speaking" aloud some very interesting words. These words were *daughter*, *cave*, *alive*, *lonely*, *lose*, and *themselves*. The words were followed by the name *Bronwen*.

Even though I still didn't trust the accuracy of the Ghost Radar®, these words were enough to keep me interested. We spent the next hour at the Hobbit house shooting video and trying to catch the voices of the dead on our audio recorders, but nothing else out of the ordinary occurred in our presence. By then it was close to midnight, and it was a long hike back to base camp. It was time for us to leave the forest.

Somewhere along the way back to base camp we made a wrong turn. We were lost for a few minutes, but Amber soon discovered what had happened. One of our trail markers had been moved and pointed us down the wrong path. Either the ghosts of Okie Pinokie had a slick sense of humor or someone unknown to us was tracking us in the woods. The mere thought of either of these choices put my senses on overload.

Amber and I had four young men (three of whom were minors) with us, and their safety was our number-one concern.

We walked slower now, scanning the woods on both sides of the trail with our flashlights for any sign of a human presence. As we came around a sharp bend in the trail, something appeared in the beam of my flashlight. Something I had a hard time wrapping my mind around. Amber and Ryan saw it, too. So did Rodney.

In the woods alongside the trail were three shimmering apparitions floating approximately a foot and a half above the ground. I now understood what Becca had seen during our daytime investigation. The apparitions lingered for a few moments, then faded out. Even though he hadn't seen them, Steve, the youngest of the four boys, started to panic. Amber and I quickly went to him. "It'll be okay," we both said, but we weren't quite sure it would be okay. We were still deep in the woods with no idea of what else we might encounter, human or otherwise. If we had been on our own, we would have stayed to investigate, but for the moment all that mattered was getting the boys safely out of the woods. Thirty minutes later we managed to do just that.

True Haunters of the Forest

We arrived back at base camp to another flurry of human activity. Sam and Becca looked pissed off. We had seen several pairs of headlights moving down the road on our way through the woods, and now Sam and Becca verified that no fewer than six different vehicles had driven through the turnaround while we were gone. One of those vehicles was still parked about twenty-five feet away from our camp. Sam told us that the occupants of the vehicle (another group of teenagers) had ventured into the woods in the opposite direction of the Hobbit house and he and Becca hadn't seen them since. He also informed us that the parade of cars through the area had pretty much been nonstop, so he and Becca had been unable to properly investigate or perform most of their experiments.

It was obvious that our teammates were none too happy about all of the interruptions. Becca asked us if we'd had better luck in the woods, but before we could answer, another group of riders on horseback moseyed up the road and approached our camp. But this group was different from the other riders we had encountered in Okie Pinokie. I recognized the riders from YouTube videos and photographs I had seen on the Internet. This was the group of riders that referred to themselves as *the true haunters of the forest.*

The riders were naturally interested in what team WISP was up to and asked if we were performing a paranormal investigation. We introduced ourselves and told them that we were in fact paranormal investigators researching the legend of Okie Pinokie. Two of the women in the group (who were obviously intoxicated) started giggling. In fact, the riders openly admitted that they were under the influence of alcohol and introduced themselves as (*ta-da!*) "the true haunters of the forest." After a long conversation, they further admitted that they enjoyed nothing more than messing with all the kids who came to Okie Pinokie to search for ghosts. As if on cue, at that moment the group of teenagers who had parked near our camp and gone into the woods returned. Upon spying the teenagers, the haunters gave us a knowing grin and said, "We've got work to do." They thanked us for the conversation and rode over to the teenagers to do what they did best: mess with the locals.

By now it was well past one o'clock in the morning, and the human activity in Okie Pinokie showed no signs of slowing down. It was time to break camp and make the two-hour drive back home. Rodney, Steve (who still looked a tad shaken), and Jordon said it was time for them to head home, too, and they thanked us for allowing them to tag along. They hopped into their car and disappeared down the road, leaving a thick trail of dust behind them.

As we packed up our gear and prepared to leave, Sam and Becca continued to express their frustrations about what they felt was a broken investigation. They felt they had let the team down. But I didn't share their frustrations. In the end, Okie Pinokie had delivered nothing less than what I had expected: an intriguing night filled with a lot of entertaining people.

The Evidence

Video evidence: Amber was able to capture a single piece of video on her camcorder, which appears to show a small, unidentified mass floating through the air. This video was captured near the Hobbit house.

Photographic evidence: No conclusive evidence of paranormal activity was captured on still camera during the investigation.

Okie Pinokie Nighttime EVP in Chronological Order of Their Capture

---

SPECIAL NOTE FROM THE AUTHOR

Many of the nighttime EVP captured during the investigation appear to be gibberish or in an unknown language, possibly even a Native American language. As such, I will do my best to present the EVP as clearly as possible, but my spelling of the words that were captured will undoubtedly be incorrect. Also, please note that all EVP were captured in the woods or while the team was investigating the Hobbit house.

---

1. On our way through the woods, an anomalous male voice is captured on audio that says, "Spooky."

2. A female voice is captured in the woods that says, "Ta ch-chi."

3. After Ryan's Ghost Radar® speaks the word "cave," a hissing male voice is captured that demands, "Get out now!"

4. While Amber is shooting video near the Hobbit house, she declares, "It's almost too dark to pick anything up." A disembodied voice is then captured that says, "Secret."

5. At the exact moment we saw the floating apparitions in the forest, a male voice is captured that says the word (or name) "Nemah."

6. After the apparitions disappear from view, approximately seven or eight anomalous voices were captured on audio. All of these voices were gibberish or in a language I have never heard before.

Conclusion

After a great deal of debate and discussion, WISP has concluded that Okie Pinokie is inhabited by what we refer to as *guardians of the forest*. We believe that most of the paranormal activity occurring in Okie Pinokie is caused by the hundreds, perhaps thousands, of spirits that dwell there. We further believe that these spirits are spectral guardians rather than the entities that we commonly refer to as "ghosts." We thus feel that the word *haunted* is incorrect as it applies to the paranormal activity occurring in Okie Pinokie.

But there are other guardians patrolling the forest as well. These are human guardians. The group of horseback riders who call themselves *the true haunters of the forest* openly admit to deriving enjoyment from "messing with the locals." But WISP believes that if push came to shove, these same riders would do everything in their power to protect the people who come to visit their forest.

Sam and Becca originally considered the human activity in Okie Pinokie as an intrusion on our investigation. They have now come to view things quite differently. When all is said and done, it isn't the ghosts of our world that keep ghostly legends alive, but the people who go in search of them. Is Okie Pinokie really haunted? Do thousands of spirits dwell in the woods, as the legend states? Well, in the end it really doesn't matter either way. What matters is that people believe that Okie Pinokie is haunted. What really matters is that people will keep coming to search for these spirits, whether they exist or not.

This is what legends are really all about.

Chapter 7

Return to Munchkinland

Investigation: Return to Munchkinland
Start date: October 31, 2010
Place: Eau Claire, Michigan

The Season of the Witch

Halloween night, 2010, was crisp and cool when the four members of WISP gathered at my home to pass out candy to the costume-clad youngsters, scare the hell out of the older kids that came a-knocking, and of course attempt to make contact with the dead. We had spent many months preparing for this night. After the neighborhood went quiet and the "normal" people were all safe inside their homes, WISP was going to return to Munchkinland to attempt something that to our knowledge no other group of Witches or paranormal investigators has ever been able to successfully accomplish: *the forced materialization of a non-biological entity (NBE).*

With a virtual armory of technological gear at our disposal and a full-blown Pagan ritual prepared specifically for this event, WISP returned to Munchkinland in Eau Claire, Michigan, to force out of hiding the ghosts that dwell there. Beyond our usual ghost-hunting equipment (IR video cameras, still cameras, digital audio recorders, and the rest), we had recently added two thermal-imaging cameras and a K2 meter to our inventory.

Yet all that wasn't enough. For what we planned, we needed two more thermal-imaging cameras and a multi-field meter. Fortunately for us, the Michiana (this is a local term used to describe parts of northern Indiana and southwestern Michigan) Paranormal Society had loaned us two of their thermal cameras, and Sam had recently completed construction of a multi-field meter that was functioning within his specifications. If we were successful in forcing the materialization of an NBE, we had all the equipment we needed to capture and preserve the evidence.

Beyond all the techno-gadgetry, to accomplish the goal successfully we would also need a variety of ritual tools we had previously prepared specifically for the return to Munchkinland, not the least of which were four wooden staffs custom made specifically for this event. The return to Munchkinland was the last paranormal investigation WISP had planned for the year, and we intended to go out with a bang. After a triple-check to make sure all of our equipment was in order, we loaded up the van and made a late-night drive to Munchkinland.

Upon arriving at our destination, we discovered something quite interesting: the dilapidated chapel on the front edge of Munchkinland's haunted grounds had undergone a total renovation. The chapel had been re-roofed; its loose, rotted trim boards had either been repaired or replaced; and the outside of the structure had been treated to a fresh coat of white paint. Even the timeworn front doors had been replaced with brand-new steel ones. But the old cemetery surrounding the chapel was exactly as we remembered it.

As I pulled the van up to the iron fence and killed the engine, I already felt the sensation of being watched. It felt as though Munchkinland itself was watching our approach and quietly waiting for what was to come. The four members of WISP sat in silence for a few moments, centering our minds and bodies before exiting the van. Then, without speaking a word, we unloaded our equipment and entered Munchkinland.

A Recipe for Science and Magic

WISP's first order of business was to locate a spot inside Munchkinland that best suited our agenda. To do so, Sam walked the burial grounds, scanning the entire area with his new multi-field meter as Becca and Amber used their psychic senses to seek out ghosts and/or pockets of paranormal activity. This was the first time Sam had used the new meter in a real-life situation, and we were all more than a little curious as to whether or not the device would function as intended.

His multi-field meter incorporated a variety of ghost-hunting technologies, including an EMF detector, an ambient temperature gauge, and an array of electro-optic sensors that were capable of sensing air density and atmospheric vibrations. It was an impressive assortment of technology in a single device, but was the multi-field unit capable of detecting the presence of paranormal activity? The answer to this question came sooner than any of us could have imagined.

As Sam walked into the center of Munchkinland, the meter started picking up some unusual readings. Two of the device's digital gauges used to register EMFs and extreme changes in ambient temperature peaked and stayed that way for well over thirty seconds. The meter was also registering fluctuations in air density, just as it was intended to do.

While all of this was going on, I set up one of our video cameras on a tripod. If any paranormal activity occurred while we were setting up, I wanted to catch it on film. Upon surveying the area where Sam was registering the strongest readings, we discovered something quite interesting. The readings were coming from the exact spot where we had introduced energy into the ground during our previous investigation of Munchkinland. Was the energy we had created almost four years earlier still active? Or was this area of

Munchkinland a natural hot spot for paranormal activity? We decided that, either way, it really didn't matter. The spot seemed to be as good a place as any to perform our ritual and attempt the forced materialization of an NBE.

Once the location had been chosen, our next order of business was to set up the rest of our equipment and prepare for the ritual. We needed to create two separate circles of protection. Once we had created the boundary of the first (or inner) circle, we would place our camcorders and thermal-imaging cameras in strategic locations around this circle to record any paranormal activity occurring in our midst. The purpose of the inner circle was to create a protective boundary between ourselves and any entity (or entities) we managed to summon.

Becca and Amber began to cast the circle by laying down a ring of salt. Salt is commonly used during magical practice to create a protective boundary and bar the entry of unwanted spirits. In our ritual, however, the purpose of the inner circle was twofold. In addition to barring unwanted entities, the inner circle was also designed to contain any entities that materialized in our presence. Until all the equipment was in place, however, the circle of salt was only a visual representation of our magic. We would charge the circle and create the second circle of protection during our ritual. After an hour and a half of work, all our electronic equipment was finally at the ready. We donned our robes, gathered our staffs, and thus in full regalia prepared to summon the ghosts of Munchkinland.

Circles of Protection

In silence, the four members of WISP approached the boundary of the inner circle. We took our places next to the thermal cameras and video recorders, which had already been placed in the four cardinal directions: east, south, west, and north. In Becca's hand was a staff fashioned from willow. Willow, which is sacred to the crone, is believed to promote psychic energies. In Amber's hand was a staff made of alder, used by magical practitioners for protection. Alder is known as the tree of fire and the wood of the Witches. In Sam's hand was a staff made from the wood of an ash tree. Ash is the wood of balance and is believed to contain the magical elements of earth and water. I held a staff made of yew, which is associated with death, rebirth, and magic. My staff was also adorned with inlays of ebony, which has proved to be an excellent amplifier of my psychic and magical powers.

Standing among the gravestones, we silently acknowledged each other's presence and the power of the magic we would soon perform. Becca and Amber, who were clothed in beautiful ritual robes they had made specifically for this night, walked the perimeter of the circle of salt as Sam and I concentrated on focusing the bubble of energy they were creating. Once the magical boundary of the inner circle had been laid, the gals went to work creating an outer circle by walking counterclockwise (or widdershins) three times outside the inner circle.

It was now time to cast our own personal circles of protection. To do so, the four members of WISP formed a spiral of energy known as a Dragon's Loop around ourselves. To understand what a Dragon's Loop is and how it functions, try to imagine what standing in the center of a whirlwind might be like. A Dragon's Loop is essentially an ever-circling flow of energy that envelops a person in an invisible cocoon of magical protection. With our protection in place and our equipment functioning normally, it was time to attempt the summoning.

Summoning the Shadows

On Halloween night, it is believed, the veils between the worlds of the living and the dead grow thin. As we began the ritual and spoke our spells aloud, I could feel what I can only describe as a million pairs of eyes watching us. If nothing else, we were attracting quite a bit of attention from the entities of the otherworld. But did WISP possess the necessary skills to force one of these entities to materialize in our presence? The answer to this question came soon enough.

With the magical energy we had created flowing all around us, the four members of WISP began chanting aloud two words: *show yourself.* We started out softly and slowly, and built the power of our voices until Munchkinland felt thick with our energy and magic. We pushed with our willpower, chanting the words over and over again. *Show yourself. Show yourself.*

Within minutes, the lights on the K2 meter sitting on the ground at Sam's feet peaked and remained that way. On the screen of the thermal-imaging camera at my side, I started seeing swirling pinpoints of light and color that the camera's readout was registering as tiny pockets of cold air. The images were beautiful beyond description. It was like watching the creation of a galaxy through a kaleidoscope. *Show yourself,* we demanded, *show yourself*, raising the power of our voices ever higher. *Show yourself!*

What happened next is difficult to describe, but I will do my best. The air around us, which only moments earlier had felt cool and light, became heavy with the sensation of an unseen presence. The air felt thick with gravity. By the looks on my teammates' faces, it was obvious that it was getting difficult for them to move and breathe. I was also having difficultly moving and breathing. The sensation was very similar to altitude sickness. Although we could see nothing in the center of our circle, the images on the thermal camera showed that the pockets of cold and light had come together to form a single mass. Suddenly we all felt a fluctuation in the energy pattern inside the circle, a pattern that was unlike anything any of us had felt before. The lights on the K2 meter were now rising and falling at an astonishing rate.

In the center of the inner circle, we were seeing what could only be described as motion trails. Something was there, but it was moving (or perhaps vibrating) too fast for us to fix our eyes on it. The air all around us turned ice-cold. The batteries of two of the thermal-imaging cameras and all but one of the camcorders simultaneously drained, and their screens went dark.

For a fraction of a second, something appeared inside the inner circle. It took form. Then, another fraction of a second later, it was gone. The air instantly felt light again, and, in comparison to the intense cold that had enveloped us, warm. Sam quickly strode over to the only camcorder that was still functioning and pressed one of the buttons, scanning back through the footage. He gestured for the three of us to join him. We huddled around the camera. Had something really materialized inside the circle? And if so, had we captured it on film?

In the camera's viewfinder, we saw a vaporous shadow appear inside the inner circle and take form before quickly dissipating and fading away into nothingness. The shadowy form was familiar to us. It was in the shape of a man.

Chapter 8

Archer Avenue: The Legend of Resurrection Mary

Investigation: Archer Avenue's Resurrection Mary
Start date: July 16, 2005
Place: Chicago, Illinois
Note from author: The investigation of Resurrection Mary is the very first investigation WISP ever performed as a team. As such, differences from the other investigations included in this book will be apparent.

The Legend[9]

Chances are you are already familiar with the legend of Resurrection Mary, Chicagoland's most famous ghost. Mary's tale is known worldwide, having inspired songs, poems, and prose, not to mention having drawn the interest of ghost hunters, psychics, and paranormal investigators for decades.

Like many other ghostly urban legends, Mary's story is a "vanishing hitchhiker" story. Strange tales of vanishing hitchhikers abound throughout the United States and most of the civilized world. Modern versions of vanishing

---

9. Research sources: Dale Kaczmarek, "Resurrection Cemetery," *Ghost Research Society*, www.ghostresearch.org/sites/resurrection/ (©2011); and "Resurrection Mary," on the Haunted America Tours website, www .hauntedamericatours.com/ghosts/ResurrectionMary/ (© 2004–11).

hitchhiker stories, as we know them today, date back to the early twentieth century, but their true origins probably date back to earlier centuries. According to folklorist Jan Harold Brunvand,[10] modern vanishing hitchhiker legends evolved from early European stories about riders on horseback.

The most common modern version of the vanishing hitchhiker story involves a driver, usually male, who stops to pick up a young woman. At some point during the drive, he discovers that his passenger has inexplicably vanished from the vehicle while it was in motion.

There are variations on this theme:

1. Before vanishing, the woman gives the driver an address as her destination. Once the woman has vanished, the driver goes to the given address in search of answers, only to be told by the vanished woman's relatives that she has been dead for many years. The most commonly given cause of the woman's death is a car accident.

2. The woman departs the vehicle as would a normal passenger, usually wearing some article of clothing she has borrowed from the driver to protect her from the elements. She then vanishes before the driver's eyes. The borrowed article of clothing is later discovered draped over a gravestone in a local cemetery.

3. Before vanishing, the hitchhiker issues a prophetic statement, usually concerning an impending natural catastrophe or great religious evil.

---

10. Brunvand, *The Vanishing Hitchhiker: American Urban Legends and Their Meanings* (Norton, 1981).

Our interest in vanishing hitchhiker stories lies within the nature of the encounter. The interaction with the ghost occurs not because the driver went looking for the supernatural, but because the supernatural came looking for him. Adding to the mystery is that the ghosts in these vanishing hitchhiker stories pass for living persons, a situation that sets up the possibility that encounters with ghosts and otherworldly entities may occur on a regular basis without our ever realizing it.

Even though vanishing hitchhiker legends are hardly uncommon, the legend of Resurrection Mary is distinctive in one way: the sheer number of credible eyewitness accounts. Sightings of Resurrection Mary began around 1928 (although some reports posit a beginning in the early 1930s) and, although they have significantly decreased in intensity and frequency over the years, they continue to this day. Mary sightings sustained a severe drop in the 1980s, a decline believed by some to be due to an extensive renovation of Archer Avenue (the stretch of road that Resurrection Mary purportedly haunts) that included the installation of streetlights. The majority of the Mary sightings have occurred during the months of December, January, and February, which coincides with the part of the legend that states Mary's death occurred in the winter. What follows is the most commonly cited account of Mary's last night on earth.[11]

Mary was a very beautiful young Polish-American woman with blonde ringlets and stunning blue eyes. On a cold winter's night in the late 1920s, Mary and her beau went out for a night of dancing at the Oh Henry Ballroom (now known as the Willowbrook Ballroom), located on Archer Avenue in

---

11. Sources: *American Hauntings* website (www.prairieghosts.com) and the Ghost Research Society website (www.ghostresearch.org).

Willow Springs, Illinois, just outside Chicago. Mary was said to have been dressed in her favorite white party gown and matching white shoes.

Sometime during the evening, Mary and her beau had a terrible fight. Vowing that she would rather walk home in the bitter cold than endure another moment in his presence, Mary left the Oh Henry Ballroom in such a rush that she left her coat behind. Upset and desperate, she began walking down Archer Avenue, where she tried to hitch a ride with a passing motorist. But she was struck by the motorist's car. Car and driver sped down the road and disappeared without a trace, leaving Mary's dead or dying body on the side of the road. She was later buried in Resurrection Cemetery, clothed in the white party gown and shoes she had worn to the Oh Henry Ballroom on the night of her tragic death.

Who was the real-life Resurrection Mary?[12] There has been speculation that the Mary of legend was one Mary Bregovy, who was killed in an automobile accident in 1934 and buried in Resurrection Cemetery. The theory that Mary Bregovy was the living counterpart to the ghost known as Resurrection Mary has, however, come under fire in recent years due to gross dissimilarities in the physical appearance of the two women and in their stories.

Even though the accident that killed Mary Bregovy occurred around the same time that the ghost of Resurrection Mary began appearing (and subsequently disappearing), it is highly unlikely that she was returning home from the Oh Henry Ballroom at the time of her death. The accident that killed Bregovy took place on Wacker Drive in downtown

---

12. Source: *American Hauntings* website (www.prairieghosts.com).

Chicago, when the car in which she was riding collided with an elevated train support. Bregovy was thrown through the windshield of the car and died instantly. This is a far cry from being killed by a hit-and-run driver on Archer Avenue in Willow Springs, which is more than fifteen miles from downtown Chicago. Photographs of Bregovy show that she had short brown hair and dark eyes, and her relatives claim that she was buried in an orchid-colored dress. Again, this is a far cry from the blonde-haired, blue-eyed, white-gowned Mary of legend.

Who Resurrection Mary was in life, we may never know. I'm certain that the debate will live as long as the legend itself. Team WISP, like other paranormal researchers, was attracted by her story. And so, our strange journey begins…

The WISP team decided to meet up at a metaphysical bookstore on Ashland Avenue in Chicago. After some previous debate on the subject of electronic equipment, I reluctantly agreed to allow the use of cameras and audio recorders for purposes of documenting our investigations and recording eyewitness accounts. I reminded the team, however, that I wanted to keep our use of electronic gadgetry to a minimum, as the whole point of our being Witches investigating the paranormal was to use our metaphysical skills and tools to research and make contact—and not rely on electronic devices to do the job for us.

After I completed a book signing and lecture at the bookstore, we all hopped into my van and, map in hand, slowly made our way through the thick Chicago traffic and managed the short trek to the town of Justice (which borders Willow Springs), down Archer Avenue, and finally to the gates of Resurrection Cemetery. We were about to get more than we'd bargained for.

Resurrection Cemetery

As we approached the entrance to Resurrection Cemetery, I immediately became unhappy about what I was seeing—the old cemetery gates had been taken down and replaced with new ones. To understand why this was upsetting to me, it is necessary to relate the chilling accounts of August 10, 1976.

It was on that date, at approximately 10:30 in the evening, that a man driving by the gates of Resurrection Cemetery witnessed a most unusual sight. He saw a young woman wearing a white party dress standing inside the cemetery and grasping the iron bars of the gates. Concerned that the young woman had accidentally been locked inside the cemetery, he stopped at the Justice Police Department and relayed what he had witnessed to the night officer. A patrol car was promptly dispatched to Resurrection Cemetery to check out the report.

Upon inspection, the cemetery was found to be dark and vacant, with no sign of the young woman. The responding officer did, however, discover something that chilled him to the bone. He noticed that two of the bars of the cemetery gate had been pulled apart. They were bent at sharp angles. But what really disturbed him was that the bars were scorched and blackened with soot. Within these scorch marks he saw what looked to be handprints that had been seared into the metal by incredible heat. Mary, it seemed, had left behind physical evidence of her existence!

But the gates had been replaced. That physical evidence was gone now. It had been my hope to be able to grasp the scorched and bent bars with my own two hands and see if I could get a paranormal impression from them. That was impossible now. Much to the protest of my teammates, I stopped the van in a no parking zone, jumped out, and approached the gates. Closing my eyes, I took in a deep breath, and with hope beyond hope, grasped two of the greenish-brown bars of the cemetery gate. Nothing. If there was ever anything imprinted into the bars that could be seen or felt, it had vanished along with the old gates. Disappointed but still determined, I got back inside the van and drove my teammates through the new gates and into the cemetery.

Resurrection Cemetery is plain and simply huge, seemingly endless. At random, I chose one of the cemetery's many asphalt arteries and turned the corner. As we drove around the first bend in the road, we saw a most curious sight: two female deer were lying in the shade of two large stone memorials just off the edge of the road. I stopped the van and grabbed my camera, hoping to snap off a few shots before the does were disturbed by our intrusion and fled. The first doe turned out to be camera shy. She quickly rose to her feet and ran deep into the cemetery. The second doe, however, seemed more than happy to simply lie in the shade of the monument and have her picture taken. As soon as the display on my digital camera revealed a picture I was satisfied with, I threw the van into drive and we continued our trek through Resurrection Cemetery.

As we drove deeper into the cemetery, the differences between the old and new sections of Resurrection's funerary grounds became obvious. To our right were the older and decidedly creepier tombstones and monuments of old Resurrection Cemetery. To our left were modern black marble monuments adorned with gold and bronze saints and angels. I found a spot where I could safely park, and the entire team exited the van. We quickly dispersed into one of the older sections and began the process of trying to pick up on any impressions of a paranormal presence.

After about twenty minutes of searching, we reassembled at the van without much to report. Amber put it best when she stated, "It just feels like an old cemetery." Satisfied that were weren't going to be able to pick up on much at Resurrection Cemetery during daylight hours, team WISP hopped back into the van and headed for Archer Avenue and Chet's Melody Lounge.

Chet's Melody Lounge

Chet's Melody Lounge, which is located across the street and catty-corner from Resurrection Cemetery, has been associated with many ghostly sightings, including visits by Resurrection Mary. Numerous unsuspecting motorists have supposedly given Mary a ride, only to have her disappear from their vehicles as soon as they passed either the gates of Resurrection Cemetery or Chet's Melody Lounge. Some motorists have even seen her entering the lounge after inexplicably vanishing from their vehicles. Those who have chased her into Chet's were always told that no one fitting Mary's description had come in to the bar.

Upon entering Chet's Melody Lounge ourselves, team WISP was greeted by a barkeep named Leslie. After setting us up with a round of beers, she disappeared into a small kitchen behind the bar to prepare us an order of deep-fried mushrooms and mozzarella sticks. Other than Leslie and team WISP, Chet's Melody Lounge was completely empty. Choosing a small table near the back of the lounge, we sipped our beers and waited for our snacks. It was very hot in Chicagoland that day, and the bar's single window air conditioner was having a hard time keeping the place cooled down.

Leslie promptly arrived with our food, and I asked her one question right away: "What can you tell us about Resurrection Mary?" A broad grin came over her face. She said she would be more than happy to share what she knew. When I told her that we were a team of metaphysical investigators researching the legend of Resurrection Mary, Leslie inquired as to the meaning of the word *metaphysical*. After we had satisfactorily answered her question, she began to talk.

It came as no surprise when Leslie informed us that inquiries about Resurrection Mary were a weekly event at Chet's Melody Lounge. "As a matter of fact," Leslie said, "there was a guy in here just a little while ago. He was having lunch with the head caretaker of Resurrection Cemetery and was asking questions about Mary for a newspaper article he was writing."

Leslie then informed the two female members of WISP that "Mary doesn't show herself to women or those who come looking for her." While I have never heard of an encounter with Mary by a ghost hunter or paranormal investigator (as opposed to the standard innocent motorist), what Leslie said about Mary not appearing to women is contrary to many reports. While it is true that men have reported the majority of encounters with Mary, reports of encounters by women are hardly unheard of. After giving us more basic information about Mary (most of which we already knew), Leslie informed us that Chet's Melody Lounge was haunted by something other than the ghost of Resurrection Mary.

On more than one occasion, Leslie reported, racked balls on the pool table (which had long since been removed) had broken by themselves, as if struck by the invisible cue of a spectral pool player. She told us that the television set mounted to the wall would sometimes turn on and off all by itself. I looked more closely at the TV and saw that the manufacturer was General Electric. I told Leslie that I used to own a GE television that did the same thing, and that it was caused by faulty wiring rather than a ghostly sitcom aficionado. Unshaken by my comment, Leslie went on to tell us about a friend of hers that would no longer go into Chet's basement after having several ghostly encounters. These encounters had occurred while the friend was fetching bar supplies from the basement when Leslie was too busy to go and get them herself. Amber asked if we could check out the basement for ourselves, but Leslie declined, citing insurance reasons.

After a few more questions and answers that bore little relevance to our investigation, we asked Leslie if there was a nearby restaurant where we could get a full meal. She pointed us to a place called Rico D's, which, she said, is directly across from the Willowbrook Ballroom (one of Mary's most famous haunts) and had really good pizza. Unsurprisingly, she informed us that Rico D's was also haunted. We thanked Leslie for her time, the beer, and the snacks, and headed for the front door.

As we were on our way out the door, I remembered something else I'd wanted to ask Leslie. I had heard of people buying drinks for Resurrection Mary and leaving them at the end of the bar for her. When I went back to the bar and asked Leslie about this, she replied that every Halloween the owner of the bar would mix a Bloody Mary and set it at the end of the bar for Resurrection Mary. Leslie also said that, yes, occasionally someone would buy a drink for Mary and leave it at the end of the bar. I couldn't resist. I ponied up $3.75 for a Bloody Mary and left it at the end of the bar for our quarry, even though I was fairly certain that it would be dumped in the sink by Leslie herself or gulped down by the town lush long before Mary could get her ectoplasmic fingers on it.

As we walked out the front door of Chet's Melody Lounge, the bright daylight was almost blinding. I snapped a quick shot of the front of Chet's with my digital camera, and then told the team that we should probably head down to the Willowbrook Ballroom and maybe Rico D's. I thought we should wait until dark before continuing our investigation. Before we could make a decision, however, Sam spotted a caretaker across the street in Resurrection Cemetery. He wanted to catch up with this caretaker and ask him a few questions. The rest of the team quickly agreed, so we hopped back in the van and began our hot pursuit. The graveyard race was on!

Back to Resurrection Cemetery

We drove through the gates of Resurrection Cemetery again, but this time we were on the hunt for the living rather than the dead. When last seen, the caretaker's dark green Ford pickup was parked alongside the road near Resurrection's eastern fence line, deep in one of the older sections of the cemetery.

The roads in that part of the cemetery are narrow and difficult to navigate, so I maneuvered the van as fast as I dared to the spot where we had spied the truck. Naturally, the caretaker and his transportation had vanished. Undaunted, I managed to get the van turned around in a small cul-de-sac in front of a mausoleum, and we headed back the way we came. After several minutes of searching, we spotted the caretaker's truck cruising away from us toward the west end of the cemetery. I hit the gas. To an unwitting onlooker, what happened next probably looked like a bad chase scene from a live-action episode of a *Scooby-Doo* mystery. The only things missing were gaudy psychedelic flowers painted on the side of the van and a talking Great Dane.

Resurrection Cemetery boasts twisting and turning roads, and I was having a hard time catching up with our quarry. It seemed that every time I would turn left, he would turn right. Every time we thought he was in front of us, he would appear behind us. After almost fifteen minutes of our chase scene, we finally caught up with the caretaker at the front of the administration building near Resurrection's main gate. As we exited the van and approached with our cameras and digital recorders in hand, we could see the apprehensive look on the man's face. The caretaker seemed to be in his late twenties and was dressed in the usual caretaker work garb. He was also sporting one of the largest gold crucifixes I had ever seen. Resurrection is a Catholic cemetery, and I didn't want to offend the caretaker or scare him off, so I hid my pentagram necklace under my shirt.

As we introduced ourselves as a team of ghost hunters researching the legend of Resurrection Mary, an amused grin came over his face. He said that although he didn't know very much, he'd be happy to share with us what little information he had. What follows are WISP's questions and the caretaker's responses in his own words.

Q. What can you tell us about Resurrection Mary?

A. To be honest with ya, everybody's been askin' about that, and, believe me, they've been movin' her grave left and right, and they've been doin' a lot of other crazy things around here, too.

Q. They've actually been *physically* moving her grave?

A. I, you know, physically—I have no idea, because [*nervous laughter*] I don't want to carry her around, or, anyway, you know what I mean? Believe me, there's been a lot of ghostly things goin' on around here. Believe me, especially for Halloween you know, so it's been nuts around here. [*WISP found this comment rather strange, considering it was the middle of July, but we decided to allow the caretaker to finish his statement uninterrupted.*] But, uh, some of the guys have been tellin' me there that she's in section Double-M over by 79th, over there by that road. So that's where she's buried. But I don't know if that's really true, though,

I have no idea, you know, because the guys around here that are seasonal like to spook ya a little bit, and, believe me, there's something about the bars sitting in the front gate, something about that she's been bendin' the gates, that she's been doin' that, so that's what's been goin' on there. Believe me, before I got here I was readin' on the computer about it, and stuff about this stuff, and, believe me, I really don't care. The ghosts here have never done anything to me so...

Q. So you've never seen anything strange or unusual happening around here?

A. I haven't seen no ghosties spinnin' around their graves or none of that kind of crap.

Q. Is there anyone else working here that has?

A. Some of the guys that been here longer than I have, they'll probably tell you more about it.

After giving us the names of some of the older, more seasoned caretakers who might be willing to talk to us about Mary (all of whom had already left for the day), the young caretaker excused himself, stating that it was almost closing time and he had to go and "kick out" the lingering visitors and mourners who were rude enough to ignore the cemetery's hours of operation. Seeing that we had obviously overstayed our welcome, I suggested to the team that we should go and check out the Willowbrook Ballroom (known as the Oh Henry Ballroom in Mary's day) and then stop by Rico D's for some food and a few drinks.

It was still warm and muggy, so the team agreed to this course of action without debate. We left Resurrection Cemetery for the second time, turned onto Archer Avenue, and managed the short jaunt to the Willowbrook Ballroom. Well, we *almost* made it to the Willowbrook Ballroom. Just as we came to the Willowbrook's driveway, a long white limousine pulled out of the parking lot in front of us, forcing me to maneuver the van onto the shoulder of the road. After a few angry shouts and rude gestures directed at the limousine driver, I edged the van back onto the road and approached the Willowbrook. Seeing the limousine, a full parking lot, tuxedos, and the bright blue taffeta of bridesmaids' gowns, we quickly deduced that the Willowbrook was hosting a wedding reception this evening, and that getting inside to investigate without an invitation was probably going to be out of the question.

Directly across the street from the Willowbrook Ballroom, however, was the old, inviting, red-brick building that housed Rico D's Italian restaurant. (As of 2011, Rico D's is permanently closed, and there's a different restaurant in the building now.) Rico D's appeared to be far less busy than the Willowbrook, so I pulled into Rico D's parking lot and brought the van to rest in a shady spot near the back of the building. Our hot and hungry team of paranormal investigators exited the van and entered the relative comfort of Rico D's. The building that housed Rico D's had once been owned by the infamous gangster Al Capone. It has a legend and ghosts of its own.

Rico D's: Dinner and a Show?

Leslie at Chet's Melody Lounge had told us that the owners of Rico D's were in the process of renovating the restaurant in an attempt to restore the building's 1920s décor and ambiance. There were obvious signs that the renovations were underway. It was also obvious that they still had a long way to go. The bar itself looked old and authentic, and the turn-of-the-century tin ceiling felt natural and inviting. The bar-room was, however, chock full of happy-hour devotees, so we quickly made our way toward the hostess station near the back of the bar and the promise of food and drink that awaited us beyond.

After giving the hostess the secret password—"We're hungry, and we'd like something to eat"—we were led down a short corridor to the dining room, which was plain and tiny. After making a quick scan of the room, the hostess informed us that there were currently no tables available in the main dining room. We could either wait in the bar until seating became available or we could be seated immediately at a table on the outdoor patio. The day was still hot, but we reluctantly agreed to the available outdoor seating. I reassured my team-mates that it would be getting dark soon, and that with darkness came the promise of somewhat cooler temperatures. Boy, was I wrong. Twilight came, but the suffocating heat lingered on, and the last dying breaths of the late-afternoon breeze failed to cool us.

I suggested that even though we weren't going to be able to get *inside* the Willowbrook Ballroom, maybe we could re-trace Mary's steps from the front door of the Willowbrook to the gates of Resurrection Cemetery. The team agreed, but one of us also felt that we needed to provide Mary's ghost with some enticement to relive her last night on earth in our company. This sounded like a good idea, but how? Just as we began discussing ideas on how to do this, our long-delayed pizza arrived. After we had finished our meal, Amber excused herself and went off in search of the ladies' room and I decided to take a walk around the patio grounds. After several minutes of random walking, I approached the wooden fence that borders the property line at the front of Rico D's. Peering over the top of the fence, I was amazed by what I saw.

The entire area surrounding the Willowbrook Ballroom and Archer Avenue glowed with an aura unlike anything I had ever seen before. This aura, an energy field that surrounds all living and supernatural things, could be felt by sensitive people during the day, but with the fall of night it was revealed in all its spectral glory. I stood entranced at the fence line for what seemed like an eternity.

After a time, however, I felt something earthly tugging at my shirtsleeve. It felt urgent. Amber was standing next to me, pulling my arm. She had a strange look on her face. She led me back to our table and asked me to sit down, then she proceeded to tell team WISP that while she was in the restroom she had experienced a very strange sensation: a sensation of not being alone in the room, a feeling of being watched by an unseen presence. It was obvious that she was pretty excited, so I decided to go to the men's room to see if I could experience anything similar. Keeping an open mind and trying my best not to be influenced by what had happened to Amber, I located the men's room, stepped inside, and locked the door. A strong sensation of not being alone in the room washed over me almost instantly. There was something in there with me. Something not of our world.

In as even a voice and tone as I could muster, I asked the unseen presence why it was here and if there was anything it wished to say to me. There was no response. Although the presence never left the room, there were no signs that it wished to communicate with me.

Eventually, I abandoned my haunted-restroom investigation and rejoined my teammates. By the time I got back to the table, the bill had been paid and team WISP was standing by, ready to continue our search for Resurrection Mary. I grabbed my keys off the table and started walking toward the door, but as I walked I got the feeling that I had left something behind. Something important. I asked my teammates to hang on for a second and returned to the table to see if I had left anything. I did a quick search among the dirty plates, napkins, and forks, but there was nothing of importance. I did, however, notice a bright, shiny penny lying on the floor at my feet. For some inexplicable reason, I felt that it was very important for me to pick it up and put it in my pocket. I have come to trust my gut instinct and intuition in such instances. I was tucking the penny into my pocket when I rejoined my teammates and we made our way back inside Rico D's and toward the front door.

As we approached the hostess station, a friendly older gentleman greeted us and asked us if our dining experience at Rico D's had been a good one. Becca and Amber took the lead and told him that although it had taken quite a while to get our food, the pizza was exceptional and well worth the wait.

Remembering what Leslie from Chet's Melody Lounge had told us about Rico D's supposedly being haunted, I stepped up and asked the man if he was the owner and if he knew anything about the ghosts that were said to haunt the place. With a smile on his face and a twinkle in his eyes, the gentleman introduced himself as Don. He was, in fact, the owner. More important, he added quite matter-of-factly, Rico D's was indeed haunted and he would be glad to talk with us about it.

It quickly became apparent that Don not only was happy to talk with us about the haunting, but he was also excited about it. He related the history of the building, a history of organized crime, murder, and bootlegging—all of which was supposedly controlled and supervised by Al Capone. He told us there were tunnels under the building that historians believe were used to hide liquor during Prohibition. Maybe they'd also been the site of assassinations. He told us that he believed that one of the ghosts that haunted the building was none other than Al Capone's aunt, an Italian immigrant named Isabel who came to the United States in the 1930s.

Don said that many of his female customers reported having strange experiences in the ladies' room, experiences that mirrored what Amber had reported. One woman told him that she'd heard an unseen woman telling her to "put Isabel's picture back up on the wall." Don said that a few days before that incident, he had taken down several framed photographs so that he could paint the walls. At the time the woman reported hearing the voice, the photographs were being stored in an upstairs room for safekeeping. The photographs were very old, Don said, and he had found them in the basement after he bought the building. He then confirmed that one of the photographs was of an Italian woman, and he believed it to be a photograph of Capone's aunt Isabel.

Don next told us about two more ghosts that haunted the building: one, who followed him around all the time, was the spirit of a young boy named Adam; another, who haunted the basement, was nicknamed Junior. When I asked Don how he knew that the ghost of the little boy was named Adam, he replied that he had previously brought in a small team of psychics to investigate the building, and they had told him about the little boy and what his name was.

Don then went on to tell us about other minor incidents that had occurred in the kitchen and the basement. Finally, he reached under the hostess stand and held up a small vial of liquid that he told us was holy water, which had been given to him by a local priest. "When the ghosts start to get out of hand," Don said, "I sprinkle some of the water inside the building, and everything settles down."

This statement elicited raised eyebrows and skeptical looks from the four of us—not because we thought that Don was lying to us, but simply because there were obvious theatrics going on. It was also obvious that Don *wanted* the building to be haunted, probably because it was good for business and gave him something interesting to talk to his customers about. We thanked Don for his time and headed for the door.

Back to the Hunt for Mary

Once we were outside, the rest of the team noticed the aura surrounding the area that I had seen earlier. We walked to a grassy spot in front of Rico D's that was directly across the street from the Willowbrook Ballroom and sat down there to discuss how we might lure Mary out of hiding.

I suggested that if we were going to retrace her footsteps from the Willowbrook to Resurrection, we should leave some sort of metaphysical trail for her to follow. It was at that moment that I got an idea: the penny. Metal is a wonderful conductor of energy, both natural and supernatural, and in addition to the one in my pocket, I had an entire roll of pennies in the van. I suggested that we magically charge the roll of pennies with energy and intent (the intent being to make contact with Mary), then leave a trail of them along the way as "metaphysical bread crumbs" for her to follow. The team agreed that this was as good an idea as any, so I went to the van and retrieved the roll of pennies.

Holding the roll of pennies in my hand, as well as the single penny from my pocket, I asked the team to wrap their hands around my own, close their eyes, and concentrate on our intent. I could feel the energy begin to build almost immediately. I began moving our hands in a circle before us, repeating the name *Mary* over and over again: first in my mind, then aloud. We built the energy stronger and stronger, higher and higher, filling the pennies with our magic and intent.

Once our magical work was done, I stuck the roll of pennies in my pocket and walked to the edge of the road directly across from the Willowbrook. Holding the single penny in my hand, I gazed at the Willowbrook and traveled back in time in my mind. I envisioned what the Willowbrook might have looked like in the early twentieth century. I envisioned a sad and lonely Mary running out the front door and into a cold and snowy winter's night ... and to her terrible fate. I opened my eyes, whispered her name, and hurled the penny across the street. The penny bounced through the parking lot and came to rest on the sidewalk near the front door of the Willowbrook Ballroom. Our work here was done. We walked to the van and began a slow drive from the entrance to the Willowbrook Ballroom to the gates of Resurrection Cemetery.

As we drove past the Willowbrook, I noticed a middle-aged man in a tuxedo standing on the sidewalk in front of the ballroom, smoking a cigarette. What was interesting was that he was standing in approximately the same place where the penny had landed and he had a very confused look on his face. His body language also suggested that he was sensing something unusual happening around him, but he was obviously unsure of what that something might be.

He suddenly looked straight down at the sidewalk, bent over, and reached for something at his feet. It had to be the penny! I was just about to stop the van and yell at him to leave it alone, when all of the sudden he jerked his hand back like he'd touched a live electrical wire and had received a shock. He stood up, threw his cigarette to the pavement, and headed for the front door of the Willowbrook. Well, I thought, if the dead hadn't picked up on the energy we put into the penny, the living certainly had.

As we drove slowly along Archer Avenue toward Resurrection Cemetery, Becca left a trail of charged pennies by tossing them out the window at regular intervals; Sam and I kept a sharp lookout along the roadside for any signs of Mary; and Amber tried her hand at automatic writing, the form of spirit communication performed by holding a pencil or pen loosely in one's nondominant hand and absentmindedly drawing large, looping circles on a sheet of paper. By doing so, it is possible that a ghost or another entity will make contact and subconsciously instruct the automatic writer to write down a series of words, symbols, or images.

We made it to the cemetery gates of Resurrection without anything unusual happening. I pulled the van into a small parking lot across the street and killed the engine. Resurrection Cemetery was closed for the day, and we knew that we weren't going to get back inside without breaking the law and risking arrest for trespassing. We decided to chance walking up the short road that led to the cemetery gates to see if we could summon the ghost of Mary there. We knew that even that much was risky, but most likely it wasn't illegal. If we were going to make contact with Mary, this was probably our best shot.

Standing outside the gates, we gathered in our little circle and took each other's hands, closed our eyes, cleared our minds, and focused on our goal: to make contact with Resurrection Mary. We built our power, our will, our intent, and our magic. We focused our energy and our minds. We opened ourselves completely to contact. We called out to Mary.

Nothing. Nothing at all. Not so much as a tingle. So we snapped a few photos, turned off the digital recorder, and headed back to the van. Filled with both satisfaction for completing our first investigation and disappointment for not turning up any evidence, we made the long and silent trip home.

Evidence

No personal experiences directly relating to Resurrection Mary were experienced by team WISP.

Conclusion

Archer Avenue and Resurrection Cemetery glow with an aura that covers the entire area with its power and light. Everywhere we went during this investigation, we were told tales of hauntings, strange goings-on, and things that go bump in the night. Of a hitchhiking ghost in a white party dress who replays her last night on Earth over and over again, trying to make things right. Are Resurrection Cemetery and Archer Avenue haunted? Absolutely. But perhaps more by the stories, the legends, and those who have come in search of her than by Mary herself.

Conclusion

The Witchcraft Connection, Part II

As we near the end of our strange journey, it is time to revisit one of the goals I set forth at the beginning of this book. This goal is and was to examine the connection between Witchcraft and the paranormal and to discover whether the Witch's metaphysical connection gives us an advantage over paranormal investigators who only incorporate scientific methods to gather and examine evidence of paranormal activity. After seven continuous years spent tirelessly examining this connection, team WISP has collectively determined that the answer to this question is *yes*, the Witch's metaphysical connection gives us a distinct advantage over ordinary paranormal investigators.

The Witch's ability to create and manipulate energy fields, combined with heightened psychic abilities, allows for a much stronger connection to ghosts and paranormal activity than science alone can attain. Once a Witch's metaphysical skills and tools have been combined with strict scientific methods and high-tech gear, the Witch becomes a hybrid investigator who is capable of much more than either the Witch or a scientist can accomplish on their own.

WISP has further determined that paranormal investigators of any level of adeptness can benefit from a basic understanding of metaphysics and the methods used to practice it. It has become clear to us that the marriage of science and metaphysics has allowed WISP to narrow the gap between the worlds of the living and the dead, and has given us a much deeper understanding of the paranormal than we could have ever hoped for had this marriage never taken place. In other words, Witches can benefit from the understanding and implementation of scientific techniques every bit as much as scientific investigators can benefit from studying and incorporating basic metaphysical skills into their investigations.

Yet even though WISP has enjoyed great success in our studies of the paranormal, I feel it is important to point out that when the four members of the team come together, something unique is created. As I mentioned earlier in this book, I believe that, as a collective team, WISP is a natural magnet for paranormal activity, and as our skills have increased, so has our ability to attract, detect, and communicate with otherworldly entities. I believe that the combination of WISP's core members is a rare and perfect mix of energy patterns that fosters natural paranormal activity.

If I've piqued your interest in learning more about basic metaphysical skills, and possibly even incorporating them into your own paranormal investigations, then you're in luck. I've already done the legwork for you, and I'm including here a list of books that I feel are good starting points for learning rudimentary metaphysics. The books I list are also light on the religious aspects of modern Paganism, so no worries if that end of things doesn't appeal to you. This recommended reading list, which follows the epilogue, covers a broad range of topics, but centers on the basics.

Epilogue
This Last Distance

I have spent the last seven years of my life searching grave-yards, houses, and stretches of roadway for ghosts and evidence of life after death. As a result, I have come to realize that, in many ways, my journey has been a spiritual one. After decades of studying metaphysics and perfecting my occult skills, investigation of the paranormal seems to have been the next logical step on my spiritual path. Collecting evidence of a haunting has never been as important to me as interacting with those who were being haunted; proving that ghosts exist was never as important to me as spending time with the ghosts.

From the time I was a small child, I've known that ghosts are real and not the whimsy of an overactive imagination. I don't need a photograph of a specter or a disembodied voice caught on an audio recording to prove to me that ghosts exist. But such evidence intrigues me nonetheless. I have no need for science to provide me with proof of life after death, but I am intrigued by the implications of such proof. I can't help but wonder how proof of life after death would change the way we live our daily lives. I can't help but wonder if such proof would enhance or diminish our earthly existence.

I have no illusions of my own mortality. I know that one day I will die, and life as I know it will cease to exist. I believe that there is something beyond this world, and that in one form or another I will live on. But what really happens after we die, no one knows for sure. The simple fact remains that one day I must walk a final road. This is a road that one day each and every one of us must walk. And when that day comes, we will all know what awaits us at the end of that final road: a last distance that must necessarily be traveled alone.

Recommended Reading

Brunvand, Jan Harold. *The Vanishing Hitchhiker: American Urban Legends and Their Meanings*. New York: W. W. Norton & Company, 2003. Originally published in 1981.

Davis, Audrey Craft. *Metaphysical Techniques That Really Work*, revised ed. Nevada City, CA: Blue Dolphin Publishing, 2004.

Doyle, DavidPaul, and Candace Doyle. *The Journey That Never Was: A Guide to Hearing God's Voice Regardless of One's Faith, Religion, or Personal Beliefs*. Ashland, OR: Foundation for Right-Mindedness, 2006.

Fortune, Dion. *Psychic Self-Defense*. York Beach, ME: Samuel Weiser, 2001.

Loux, Michael J. *Metaphysics: A Contemporary Introduction*, third edition. New York: Routledge, 2006.

Loux, Michael J., and Dean W. Zimmerman, eds. *The Oxford Handbook of Metaphysics*. Oxford: Oxford University Press, 2003.

Monroe, Robert A. *Far Journeys*. Garden City, NY: Doubleday, 1985.

———. *Journeys Out of the Body*. New York: Broadway Books, 2001. First published by Doubleday in 1971.

O'Neill, J. F. *Foundations of Magic: Techniques & Spells That Work*. St. Paul, MN: Llewellyn Publications, 2005.

Penczak, Christopher. *The Mystic Foundation: Understanding and Exploring the Magical Universe*. Woodbury, MN: Llewellyn Publications, 2006.

———. *The Witch's Shield: Protection Magick & Psychic Self-Defense*. St. Paul, MN: Llewellyn Publications, 2004.

Todeschi, Kevin J. *Edgar Cayce on the Akashic Records*. Virginia Beach, VA: A. R. E. Press, 1998.

Appendix

Witchcraft is an ancient practice with strong ties to its modern-day adaptations, commonly known as Wicca and Neopaganism. Modern Witchcraft is a life-affirming, nature-based belief system based upon the reconstruction of pre-Christian traditions, many of which originated in Ireland, Scotland, and Wales. Many practitioners of modern Witchcraft honor both the male and female aspects of Deity and draw upon a pantheon of gods and goddesses. Witches manipulate energy by casting spells in hopes of perpetuating a specific outcome, such as healing or protection. A Witch's spells are similar to the prayers used in Christianity and other religions, in which the spoken word and a series of gestures are used to create change on a personal or even a global level.

To Write to the Author

If you wish to contact the author or would like more information about this book, please write to the author in care of Llewellyn Worldwide, and we will forward your request. Both the author and publisher appreciate hearing from you and learning of your enjoyment of this book and how it has helped you. Llewellyn Worldwide cannot guarantee that every letter written to the author can be answered, but all will be forwarded. Please write to:

Marcus F. Griffin
⁒ Llewellyn Worldwide
2143 Wooddale Drive
Woodbury, MN 55125-2989

Please enclose a self-addressed stamped envelope for reply, or $1.00 to cover costs. If outside the USA, enclose an international postal reply coupon.

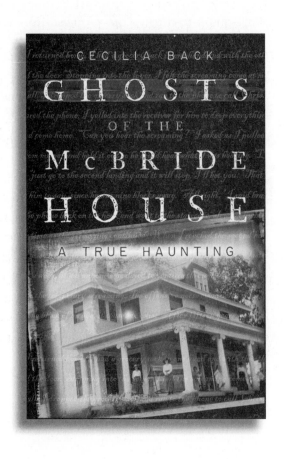

CECILIA BACK

GHOSTS
OF THE
McBRIDE
HOUSE

A TRUE HAUNTING

Ghosts of the McBride House
A True Haunting
CECILIA BACK

It took Cecilia Back only a few weeks to confirm that her new home—a Victorian mansion just across the street from a historic military fort—was haunted. But instead of fleeing, the Back family stayed put and gradually got to know their "spirited" residents over the next twenty-five years.

Meet Dr. McBride, the original owner, who loves scaring away construction crews and the author's ghost-phobic mother. Try to catch sight of the two spirit children who play with Back's son and daughter and loud, electronic toys in the middle of the night. Each ghost has a personality of its own, including one transient entity whose antics are downright terrifying.

Despite mischievous pranks, such as raucous ghost parties at two a.m., the Back family have come to accept—and occasionally welcome—these unique encounters with the dead.

978-0-7387-1505-6, 216 pp., 5³⁄₁₆ x 8 $14.95

To order, call 1-877-NEW-WRLD
Prices subject to change without notice
Order at Llewellyn.com 24 hours a day, 7 days a week!

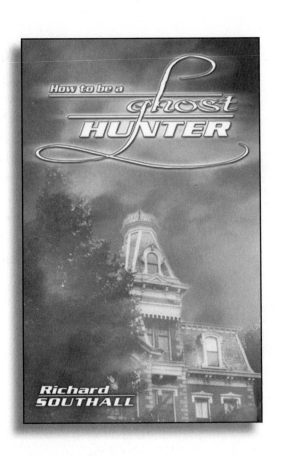

How to be a *ghost*
HUNTER

Richard
SOUTHALL

How to Be a Ghost Hunter

RICHARD SOUTHALL

So you want to investigate a haunting? This book is full of practical advice used in the author's own ghost-hunting practice. Find out whether you're dealing with a ghost, spirit, or an entity ... and discover when you should stop what you're doing and call in an exorcist. Learn the four-phase procedure for conducting an effective investigation, how to capture paranormal phenomena on film, record disembodied sounds and voices on tape, assemble an affordable ghost-hunting kit, and form your own paranormal group.

If you have some time and a little money to spend on equipment, this book will help you maintain a healthy sense of skepticism and thoroughness while you search for authentic evidence of the paranormal.

978-0-7387-0312-1, 168 pp., 5³⁄₁₆ x 8 $12.95